Looking For You, Finding Me

The joy and sorrow of an adoptee as she searches for her family of origin

Rebecca Erickson

Cover design by: Brad Fitzgerald

First Print Edition: July, 2020

ISBN: 979-8-6570-1974-2

Dedication

This book is dedicated to my precious husband, Tom DeCicco, who has supported me in getting this finished, to my late husband, Jon Erickson, who walked with me through the journey and nagged me to write it down, and to you, the reader, who shares my journey.

Preface

Today with the advent of DNA searches, more and more adopted people are looking for their families of origin. When I found mine, that was not the case but some things are always the same. Finding family leads to life changing decisions, vulnerability on both sides and the possibility of wholeness that can be found no other way.

This is the story of my life as I know it. Some of it comes from my own memories, some from the memories of others, some from speculation, and maybe some is even pure fiction—I can't say for sure. Memory is a funny thing; it shifts and adjusts to allow us to fill in the gaps or perhaps to jump over them entirely. You may begin to research and say, "But that can't be! No such train ever left from that place at that time!" Or in another place you may say, "I am sure that is not at all how that happened. I was there and that is not how I remember it." But this is my story, the one I lived and live today: The one that would build me into the woman I am, the story that moves and sustains me. I share it with you in all humility and because I must. It is a story of grace, the hand of God moving through lives and through time to bring about miracles of healing and wholeness.

It is the story of the love of Jesus Christ for his precious lambs—every one of us. I hope you will read without judgment concerning times and places. I pray you will read with an open heart and be blessed.

Jesus said, "I have come that they may have life and have it to the full." John 10:10

Step by step, He moved me from fear to fullness.

Acknowledgments

No book happens in a void. This book has taken years and a community to come into being.

Without the cooperation, love, and support of all my siblings, this story would never have been written. I love you dearly.

The writers' group I belong to, especially the leader Cynthia Fabian, helped me to believe this story could become a book.

And, I am deeply indebted to those friends who have read the manuscript, some over and over again, helping smooth the rough edges. You know who you are. I would name you but I fear I might leave someone out and that would never do. Thank you all.

To my children, who have always believed in me, I just want to say that I believe in you. You are all so gifted. Now is the time to follow your own dreams.

Annette Bergman, my dear friend, fellow writer and greatest supporter, there are no words of gratitude that can possibly express my thanks to you. You made it happen!

Finally, my editor, who chooses to remain unnamed, deserves a medal for skill, patience, and fortitude. Thank you.

1

I Will Tell Her, I Won't

I sit at the table, my best note paper before me, ripping the hang-nail from my right index finger with my teeth. A tiny drop of blood falls on the page. "Dang! Now I can't use that one!" I exclaim crumpling the paper and throwing it on the floor where three others already lie. *I should probably just do a draft on notebook paper first before I run out of my good paper. I just want to be prepared for the meeting.*

I am an adopted child. Well, no longer a child, but adopted when I was one, and as good as my life has been I have never felt quite complete. *Who am I –really?* My adoption was unusual in that I was basically taken from my mother's arms without her previous knowledge and against her will.

Today I am about to meet my biological sister. She will be the first sibling I have ever met. The thing is, I know she is my sister but she doesn't know I am her sister.

I sigh, looking at the paper. *Maybe this isn't something I can write to her after all. And anyway, I might not even want to reveal who I really am.* Absent mindedly I reach for the coffee cup in front of me and take a big gulp. "Oh, yuck! This is horrible! It's cold!" Giving up on the whole idea of being prepared, I get up, take my coffee cup to the sink and look at the clock. It's later than I thought. I reach for my coat.

It's time!

* * *

"I will tell her...I won't tell her...I will tell her...I won't tell her"

The words beat an uncertain rhythm that plays in my head matching my hesitant footsteps as I make my way down the long corridor of the nearly deserted Warren Mall in Warren, PA. Like so much of Warren, the Mall was once new, bright, filled with stores and busy with shoppers, but now the walls of the mall are dingy. Gated doors cover empty store fronts looking like toothy gaps between the few existing businesses.

It is Wednesday, October 11, 1995, and I am about to meet my sister for the first time.

Will I tell her I'm her sister? If I do tell her, am I up to facing whatever the opening of that door would bring?

Terrified by both the fear of what I may learn and what I might do, I make my way toward one of the few places still open in the mall, the place Donna had chosen. It is a pedestrian little place with a counter, and a single row of booths with only cheap chrome napkin holders for table decoration. Their mainstay is coffee and hotdogs.

I would have liked to meet somewhere worthy of a grand event, a place with tablecloths and folded napkins—in case I choose to unveil the truth—but she isn't interested in meeting a stranger in a classy place. If she is going to meet someone she doesn't know and might not care for it is better to meet in a place easy to escape from—and no place would be easier to walk out of than that place!

2

Fifteen Thousand Friendly People

As I walk down the mall corridor, I wonder: *How could the secrets surrounding my adoption have stayed buried in this small town all these years, fifty years to be exact?*

I catch a glimpse of myself in a store window as I walk past; a middle-aged woman with short blonde hair. What happened to the young woman with mid-length brown hair I was not so long ago?

My blonde hair is a byproduct of being a beautician. I wonder what color hair my sister has? Maybe gray—we are old enough for gray hair. Or maybe she colors hers as well? Will her eyes be brown like mine? I wonder if she is short like I am? In all the years I have been searching for her, have I ever seen her before? Passed her in this very hall and didn't know? It's a small town, anything is possible. I wonder if I am going to faint?

Warren, Pennsylvania, where I, where we, were raised is a town built in a valley with the Allegheny River running through it. Those with "old wealth" live in stately homes built along the valley floor but out of the reach of the river when it floods. The rest of us live in houses that crawl up the hillsides and cling there in neighborhoods once defined by family groups.

In the late 1800s, new immigrants built houses next to brothers or cousins who had arrived a few years before hoping to find some sense of safety and

3

belonging. Thus, neighborhoods were often ethnic in early 1900.

By 1945, when I arrived, the neighborhoods were beginning to be defined more by economics than by family groups, with the exception of the many Italian families that had settled together on the West End of town where the Allegheny River overflows its banks, flooding yards and often homes every spring when the ice begins to break up.

The blessing of the floods is that, along with the damage they do, they leave behind rich soil when the waters recede, soil perfect for gardening. Everyone envies the Italians their beautiful vegetables and flowers. But in the 1940s, 50s, even into the 60s, the Italians were often eyed with suspicion. They were darker skinned than those of European descent who lived on the East Side of town and many of the first-generation immigrants still spoke Italian at home.

How well I remember being a child of nine or ten. Mom took me, along with my little brother and sister, venturing across the tracks to a greenhouse tucked into one of the Italian neighborhoods to buy plants for the garden. There was nowhere else on earth, at least our part of earth, where such healthy, lush vegetable and flower plants could be found.

"Now don't be wandering around. Stay close to me!" Mom whispered at us nervously.

I wasn't afraid of Italians. My best friend and next-door neighbor, Jill, had an Italian dad and I loved him. Jill and I spent lots of time at her Italian grandparents' home. They always welcomed me with open arms and plenty of food.

Grandma Bova would look at my thin little body and insist, "Eat, Eat! You too skinny!"

Then she would go on and on in her wonderful Italian/English that was impossible for me to understand but Jill understood just fine. Mom never minded when I went with Jill to visit them. They didn't live on the West End.

No, it wasn't the people who scared me—it was the place, as though we had entered a dangerous foreign country and needed to be wary once we had crossed the tracks to the West End.

The train tracks ran across a bridge over the Allegheny River just west of the downtown. The train station was located on the east side of the tracks—everything across the tracks was considered "The West End." The prejudices of the town ran deep. At one time at the east entrance to Warren there was a sign telling blacks to "move on." Terms of racial bias were used to refer to the Black people and the Italians in our area. Thinking about it today leaves me horrified, angry and sad, but even as a child I knew it was wrong and I hated it when I heard anyone use such terms. Yet, a sign at the north entrance to the community read; "Welcome to Warren, the home of 15,000 friendly people."

With trembling knees and covered in a light sweat that is making me feel both hot and cold, I walk past the many vacant store fronts in the mall.

What am I getting myself into?

I saw the neighborhood where Donna's parents live, I wasn't impressed. It isn't far from the railroad tracks. How is it that railroad tracks have the power to divide a town? If I reveal myself, can we keep the secret any longer? Who will judge me? How will I be judged? When did I become such a snob? I hate this!!

What am I getting myself into?

Most people in Warren have lived in the same place for years. Neighborhoods feel safe. People know one another with every kid belonging to everyone in the neighborhood, at least that's how it was in my neighborhood when I was growing up.

"Stand up straight, Becky," Jill's mom would yelp at me as she whacked me on the back to correct my teen slouch.

I wasn't offended. I expected to be yelled at or fed by the neighbors. It all seemed so open, so honest to me as a child.

Sometimes though, I overheard adults whispering as they huddled around a kitchen table. The talk stopped when any kid entered the room. It seemed knowledge itself was divided. There were those who knew and those who were never to know.

The divide wasn't only between places, and between those who knew things and those who didn't, there was also a division in lifestyles.

Back then, nearly every major street corner boasted a church. I loved walking by Holy Redeemer, the Catholic Church on the corner of Pennsylvania Avenue and Russell Street, my street, the East End of town. As I child I thought it was odd to have a Catholic church on the East End because I thought most Catholics *were Italian* and that all Italians *were Catholic.* If most of the Italians lived on the West End, why was the only Catholic Church on the East End? *What did I know? I was a kid!* When the heavy doors opened and the faithful entered or departed, the musky scent of incense would waft out carrying a hint of holy mystery with it, intriguing this Evangelical Covenant, thoroughly Protestant child.

There were just as many dark bars as there were bright churches. The stench of sloshed beer, overflowing urinals, cheap smokes and rank sweat rushed out from doors propped open, either in welcome or just to let in a bit of air and light. *Good* people walked by quickly and didn't look in, except to sneak a quick peek, hoping to catch some holier-than-thou neighbor or church member bending an elbow.

High on the hillsides, in the deep wooded areas, the very poor lived in shanties. Public health nurses and a few school teachers were the only ones who knew or cared about them. What was out of sight basically did not exist to spoil our lovely community.

It was into this community of contrasts that I had arrived in May of 1945 at the tender age of 6 weeks, the adopted child of Dorothy and Milton Samuelson.

"I am my Mommy's and my Daddy's adopted darling," I would proudly announce from the time I was about 18 months old. Oh, I knew I was very special! I was wanted. I was loved. My life was safe and secure, the way a little child's life should be.

But there has always been a part of me that just somehow feels incomplete.

As I grew older, I was so sure I had a twin that I would relentlessly pester my poor mother to learn more about who I *really* was. In various flights of fancy, I imagined myself to have Native American blood, or perhaps Jewish. Once I declared I was sure I was part Black. Mom adamantly assured me I did not have a twin nor did I have the blood of any of the above peoples! How disappointing. I wanted to be a twin with Native American, African, and Jewish roots. But no matter how persistent I was in my pestering, Mom would tell me nothing except what I *was not* and that I was born in Denver, Colorado and that was *all* she knew. Mom was never a good liar, so even as she spoke, I sensed there was more to the story, but she wasn't about to reveal *the secret*.

3

The Secret Begins To Unravel

It is not until the winter of 1988 that the first threads of *the secret* begin to unravel.

It is hard to get a speaker for Christian Women's Club to come to Warren when the roads are icy, so I have been asked to speak. I live in town. It saves the club from worrying about road conditions and spares them mileage expenses.

I begin, saying, "I am adopted. I was born in Denver, Colorado and when I was 6 weeks old Dorothy and Milton Samuelson adopted me. I am blessed."

A hundred or so women listen intently as I speak. My voice quivers a little.

This is strange. I don't normally feel so nervous. It must be because I'm talking to people who have known me all my life. This is much harder than sharing my story with strangers.

It certainly isn't the fact that it's a large group. I'm used to speaking with large groups, but these women know me, know Mom. Several are Mom's close friends, friends from high school—forever friends, who have come to hear me tell the story of how God has worked and is still working in my life.

My testimony is always the story of my adoption and of God's provision in our lives after Daddy died, but today I'm telling it in my home town, and Mom is here.

After the meeting the women stand in line to talk with me. It's always this way after I speak. Women want to know more about God who is a loving Father. So many have only known angry fathers and a fierce God. But today it's Mom's friends who crowd the line and they are more interested in me than in God.

"Your story is amazing, Becky!"

"I didn't know you were born in Denver!"

"God certainly has had his hand on you."

"You ought to be a minister, Becky." (I hear that often and it always makes me laugh!)

Eventually, the line thins and finally comes to an end. Mom and I pack up my stuff and walk to my car. I barely manage to shut the car door when Mom turns to me and in a strangled voice says, "Becky, I wish you wouldn't have told about being born in Denver. I have never told anyone that—even my best friends!"

Over the years, I have begged Mom to tell me more about myself but what I have shared today is all she has ever shared with me, and now she's scolding me for saying I was born in Denver?

"Well, Mom," I reply impatiently, "I hardly think my birth mother is going to hear that story all the way from Denver but if she does and if she should try to contact me, then it must be God's will! Besides, this is the testimony of God's faithfulness and I feel I have to tell it."

My usually warm, supportive mother huddles against the passenger door, chilling the car with her silence. I drive her home. When we get there, instead of inviting me in or kissing me goodbye, she gets out of the car without a backward glance and goes into the house. Her back is ramrod straight. A sure sign she is fighting to keep control.

I drive away, angry, puzzled and deeply hurt.

Then it's February 1989. *Where did the past year go?* I wonder. Mom has softened and returned to her usual self. I am thankful, especially thankful because Mom is scheduled to have surgery and I don't want any ill feelings between us. She is just 74 years old.

Several years ago, she had a heart attack but her recovery has been good.

She entertains a lot, works in the garden, mows the lawn and is the primary caregiver for my step father, Dave, now 79, as his health steadily fails. We have all noticed how she tires so much more quickly.

Dad, as I have called my step father for many years now, had heart by-passes followed by nine strokes a few years ago. He's no longer able to drive the car. That's hard for him because he's a take-charge sort of man.

While he can no longer hunt or walk in the woods due to his failing health, a true frustration for a retire PA Game Protector, he still putters in his garden and the lawn and landscaping are a point of pride for him. Being a perfectionist, he doesn't trust anyone but Mom to mow their lawn *properly*. But this past summer, Mom has found it more and more difficult to keep up with the daily tasks, much less doing the yard work.

As I think of Mom and yard work, I think of her hair because somehow in my mind, hair seems connected with so many major event in our lives.

Mom's hair is still its original youthful blonde color, thanks to Miss Clairol®, but even Miss Clairol can't do anything about its fine texture! Her hair has been the bane of her existence because as soon as she gets too warm, or near humidity, or heaven-forbid, caught in the rain, it collapses against her head like dandelion fuzz plastered to her scalp. And for Mom, hair is, always has been her crowning glory—and the lawn mowing is more than just exhausting, it is hair destroying!

A recent visit to her heart doctor reveals a leaky heart valve. He has advised a valve replacement, a surgery he reassures her "is very successful these days."

"I am really uncomfortable about having this surgery, Becky," Mom confides in me, "but because Dad needs me, I guess I had better." So, she has reluctantly agreed to go ahead with the operation.

In technical terms Mom's surgery is deemed "successful" because the new valve works as it's supposed to. However, because her brain was deprived of oxygen during surgery, Mom has never walked or spoken anything understandable since.

With great sadness, the family agrees she must be placed in a nursing home. It was because of this I finally hear *the secret.*

4

Virtually Kidnapped

My Aunt Margaret has three great loves: Jesus, talking, and her family in just about that order. She and Mom went to high school together and became such close friends their classmates called them "The twins." There was nothing they didn't share. Eventually, Margaret married Mom's brother, making them sisters-in-law as well as best friends.

I love my aunt and now that Mom can no longer speak, Margaret has become my surrogate mother. Because she's a shut-in due to health challenges, every week I drive to her house, do her hair, share a cup of coffee or tea, and spend time sharing our burdens, our memories and laughter.

This fateful day I'm giving her a permanent. It's a long, smelly process.

Is it spending all that time? The ammonia fumes? Or God himself that has causes her to speak the unspeakable?

"Becky," she says as I stand behind her winding her hair around the rollers, "try not to judge your mom. I know this will be a shock to you but this is something I feel I must tell you. I begged your mom to tell you but she wouldn't. Now she can't. I have prayed and prayed about it and I feel the Lord wants you to know. I need to tell you before something happens to me and then there will be no one to tell you your story.

"Milton and Dorothy got married in 1936. She was so sweet and pretty: five foot four, with fine blond hair, carefully arranged in a twist at the back of her head, and little curls always escaping, much to her chagrin," Margaret adds with a chuckle. "Your mom envied me because I had jet black hair that looked good even when it was tousled and windblown. I want you to understand, Dorothy was naive and trusting. Those blue eyes of hers sparkled when she was happy and overflowed with tears when she was not. It was impossible for her to hide her emotions. Milton was a little taller than Dorothy with dark hair and hazel eyes that sported a wicked gleam when he was teasing her. When they looked at one another, the joyous intimacy that leaped between them was so powerful it made the rest of us turn our eyes aside."

Margaret continued. "They married when she was 21 and he was 26. They couldn't wait to start a family but Dorothy didn't get pregnant easily. After a few years of false hopes and dashed beliefs that *this is finally it,* they found out she was pregnant. They were overjoyed! But the baby was spontaneously aborted. Then, to add to the pain, the doctor delivered shocking news. Dorothy had abdominal tuberculosis and would never be able to carry a child. Your mom wept for days. We all felt so terrible. No one knew how to comfort her. Milton was nearly beside himself.

"More than anything else, your mom wanted to be a mother so she and Milton applied to adopt a baby. There were many roads to adoption in those days, some official and above board and others questionable. Honey, your adoption was *secretive*, privately arranged, a virtual kidnapping."

The words *virtual kidnapping* ring in my ears. The parents I knew would never be part of anything the least bit shady. How could that be?

I continue rolling my aunt's hair, my brain in shock, my hands doing their well-practiced job.

I feel removed, as though I have been abducted to some foreign place. I can hear my aunt's voice but I don't grasp her words. Then I realize she is going on with the story and I connect once more.

"In the fall of 1944, Dorothy and Milton received word through a Covenant pastor that a baby would be available for adoption about the end of March. The pastor was serving in Warren when your mom lost her baby. He had since moved to the church in Erie, PA. I am not sure how he became involved but somehow the family of your birth mother's husband learned about Dorothy and Milton and decided they would be good parents for you.

"They interviewed your mom—I don't remember that Milton was along...maybe he was working—in their prestigious home to see if she and Milton would meet their requirements to be the parents they sought for this baby who would be born-out-of-wedlock. They made it perfectly clear that this was a shame that must never reflect on their family. Could Dorothy and Milton keep *the secret* as long as they lived? Dorothy told me after the interview that she had broken into a cold sweat, shivering with horror at the thing they were being asked to do. She knew it wasn't right, yet above all else, she wanted this baby."

Aunt Margaret looks out the kitchen window, her eyes on the painful distant past she's reliving in order to bring my life to me. She is silent for several minutes, then she continues.

"Eventually and with a quivering voice, your mom told me later she assured them that she and Milton would tell no one aside from Jim and me because she and Milton would need our help. She also absolutely promised them that *we* would never breathe a word concerning the baby's origins. Based on this secretive arrangement, the family finally approved the upcoming adoption.

"Believe me," Aunt Margaret said, "the family of your birth mother's husband was well placed and highly thought of in Warren. And they could, when necessary, *make things happen* and your birth mother's pregnancy had made it necessary. I certainly can understand how that poor woman ended up pregnant. The family didn't tell your mom the story but eventually we learned what had happened."

Almost without stopping to breathe, Aunt Margaret rushes on with the story, as though fearing if she doesn't keep talking until she gets it all out, the ghost of the past will haunt her forever.

"It was war time, 1944. Your birth mother's husband had not been sent overseas to fight but was stationed in Denver, CO. While he was there, he fell in love with another woman and wrote to your birth mother telling her he wanted a divorce. Humiliated and filled with rage she scribbled off her reply, 'Never! I will never give you a divorce! We have two kids and no other woman is going to have you, at least not legally!' In order to even the score, she found a lover of her own. But then she got pregnant."

By now, I have the perm-rods all wrapped and the solution on her head. We have some time to wait while the processing takes place. I sit down at the kitchen table, my knees trembling, my head aching. The way I thud into the chair seems to snap my aunt out of her reverie.

"Oh, my goodness!" she exclaims. "Look at the time. You must be starved. I'm going to put on the coffee pot. There are some plums on the counter over by the sink and I made some egg salad sandwiches. I'll get them from the fridge. I think we have time to eat while I process, don't we? I'll finish this story after we have fortified ourselves. Are you alright? This must be hard for you to hear. I am sorry your mother couldn't bring herself to tell you long ago."

I set her kitchen timer for the processing time. We make a feeble attempt at small talk but the story of my life refuses to wait politely for lunch to be done. Between bites and sips, Aunt Margaret continues.

"Dorothy was 30, Milton was 35. They were so excited that at long last they would have a baby. They couldn't stop talking about you. Of course, they didn't know if the baby would be a boy or a girl but it didn't matter. I was hoping it would be a little girl.

"The family of your birth mother's husband wrote to him and told him to come get her. That's why you were born in Denver. After you were born, we learned you were a tiny girl. It would be six weeks before we would meet you. On Monday, May 7, your parents got a call that you and your birth mother had gotten passage on a train to Erie. You would arrive May 13. It was a long exciting week while we waited. Finally, on Sunday, Jim drove the four of us to Erie.

"When we got to Erie, the pastor and Jim went to meet the train. Dorothy, Milton and I waited with the pastor's wife at the parsonage. Your birth mother was not to see your parents so there would be no chance she would recognize them later in Warren. Jim and I didn't live in the area at that time, so Jim was permitted to go along to hold you while the pastor drove back to the parsonage. It was a privilege he would regret the rest of his life."

The timer rings startling both of us.

"We have to get this solution rinsed out of your hair…now," I tell her. "When I was in beauty school, I learned this stuff can weaken your hair and it can all break off if it's left on too long. I sure don't want you to end up with a crew cut," I say, trying to lighten the mood a bit.

"Oh, I think I would look quite chic with a crew cut," she answers as she moves to the sink. "Anyway, I trust you completely, Becky. We have a special bond. We always have. You were the little girl I could never have. I suppose that's why I am telling you your story. I can't hide it from you any longer."

I finish up the perm and begin to style her hair. It is still mostly black and full. My mom still envied it right up until the time of her surgery. While I style her hair, Aunt Margaret is finishing up her/my story.

"That day, May 13, 1945, was Mother's Day. The pastor's wife presented your mom with her first Mother's Day corsage. The pastor presented her with her first child. She took you in her arms and cried. Milton put his arms around both of you and sobbed.

"We stayed at the parsonage that night. Your mom and dad were much too excited to sleep. They couldn't wait for the day when they could take you home with them.

"When Jim and I were finally alone in a bedroom with the door closed, he wept. I thought he was weeping tears of joy for Dorothy and Milton, or maybe tears of sadness because we would never be able to have children due to my health, but eventually he sobbed out to me, 'I hope that I will never live to hear another woman's wrenching cry as her child is taken from her. The memory of that sound will haunt me forever.'

"Monday, Jim drove us back to Warren. You were left with the minister and his wife. Because your birth mother had never agreed to give you up for adoption and her husband had never signed any papers, you were kept at the parsonage long enough to legally be declared an *abandoned baby* and then adopted under that clause. You certainly were not abandoned. You arrived with a suitcase full of lovely dresses and bonnets. In reality, you were a kidnapped baby, taken from a woman who was helpless before the power of those who were determined to do-what-is-right and brought back to the very town in which she lived. Honey, you have grown up here, going to the same schools as your half-siblings.

"Your birth mother's husband eventually came home from the service. He and she attempted to put their lives back together.

"Despite the fact that Jim and I had planned never to return to Warren, we did return and opened a little grocery story not far from the house where your birth mother and her husband lived.

"I came to know your older sister. I don't remember her name. She was a chatty little girl who loved to visit with me at the store, a child starved for love and attention. When I learned that her mother was going to have another baby, I was thrilled for her and told Dorothy about it—thinking it would make her happy, as well, that the mother who had lost her child and made Dorothy's life so rich and joyful was once again going to have a baby to hold.

"But Dorothy wasn't happy. She was fearful and angry. 'You are not ever to speak of that woman. We are not supposed to know her or anything about her. *Do Not* ever speak of her again,' she said severely.'"

"And, Becky, I have never told a soul until today. The thing is, I have buried this so deeply that I can't remember what your birth mother's name is. I have tried and tried but it just won't come!"

At last she is quiet. This final bit of information leaves me completely undone. I am unable to move, unable to think.

Eventually, I pack up my bag, putting away scissors, my smock and the cape I have had around her. I put the combs and brushes into their proper places in the old train case that I have converted into a traveling hair salon. I do all this without knowing I am doing it. The snap of the latch reminds me my job here is finished. Steeped in sharp, eye-watering ammonia fumes and shocking news, I prepare to leave.

As I open the front door, Aunt Margaret calls after me, "If I remember your birth mother's name, I'll call you."

5

Her Name Is Grace

I pull into our driveway going too fast and nearly hit the side of the garage. I hurry into the house, frantically calling to my husband, "Jon! Jon!"

He comes running. Taking one look at me he says, "Sit down before you fall down."

I quickly sit down.

"What's wrong?" he asks in alarm.

In hysterical sobs I tell him what I know.

"I'm furious with Mom. How could she have known all this time and *lied to me*! Didn't she trust my love enough to know I would love her even if I found my birth mother?" I wail.

Jon looks at me astonished and completely baffled but before he can ask any questions, I continue with my tirade.

"Her lie is a betrayal of all the love and trust I thought we shared. Jon, I'm 44 years old. My world isn't at all what I thought it was. I don't even know who I am!" I sob.

Jon finally calms me down enough that I am able to tell him what has happened to me since I left the house only 3 hours before.

Somehow, I fix supper. We eat. Jon's father, who lives with us, looks at my ravaged face but wisely doesn't ask any questions. As the three of us are cleaning up the supper mess, the phone rings. It's Aunt Margaret.

"Becky, I remembered her name. When I had my hands in the dishpan doing the dishes, it came back to me!"

"Don't tell me," I shout into the phone. "I'll drive down. I'll be there in less than five minutes!"

"Do you want me to go with you?" Jon asks. "Are you all right to drive? You are so upset and it's dark out"

"I'll be ok. I just need to do this alone."

He nods, hugs me and hands me my coat. "Be careful and remember no matter what you have learned today, you are still the *same* wonderful girl I married and love."

I arrive at my aunt's home in minutes. Although we usually drink coffee, she has hot water on for tea.

"Tea just seems more soothing," she explains. "It's herbal."

We sit at the kitchen table, our steaming cups held in hands that tremble slightly.

"Becky, your mother's name is Grace Bennod. Her husband's name is Norton. I don't know if they still live in the area or are even alive."

"Where is your phone book?" I ask, jumping up and rummaging through her kitchen drawers.

"It's in there, in that marble top thing right around the corner." She directs me toward the living room.

I find it and fumble through the pages while she pulls her chair next to mine so she can see too.

"Bennod, Norton, Sr. It's here—address, phone number..."

It is not one of the more prosperous areas of Warren. I am uncertain. I can't imagine what I can do with this information. Suddenly, I realize I can't do anything without causing a possible catastrophe in the life of the woman who had given life to me. The name in the book is that of Grace's husband.

Is she still living? Her name is not listed. What if I call or go to visit and her husband answers the door? How would he react? I don't know what he is like. Would he cause a scene, divorce her, beat her? What about the siblings my aunt said I have? Do they even know I exist? I have a wonderful life. Do I have the right to go barging into someone else's life perhaps sending it spiraling downward to who knows what ending? And what are they like? What sort of Pandora's Box might I be opening if I try to contact them?

I sit staring at the name in the phone book, stunned, feeling like a mouse cornered by a rattlesnake undulating before it, waiting to strike and eat.

Pale and shaky, I drive home and walk into my husband's arms.

"My mother's name was or is Grace Bennod. Her husband is Norton," I tell him.

"Becky, if that's true, I went to school with your brother, Norton Jr. He went by Norrie. I am sure if you look in the scrapbook my mother made for me you will find him in the fourth grade picture."

I hurry to the bookcase where our albums are kept and pull out Jon's scrapbook. Together we turn pages until we find the fourth grade picture.

"There he is!" Jon points to a boy who looks just like our son.

I begin to cry.

All these years I have wondered what my family looks like, what characteristics and features our children have that come from my genetics. We all have agreed that our son Jonny looks a lot like Jon but there is something about the shape of his face that's not quite like Jon's. People sometimes tell me, "Jonny looks like you," but I can't see it. However, here, in a photo so clear there was no mistaking it, I see my family in our son. His face is shaped just like my brother Norrie's. And like mine!

* * *

Now I am on my way to meet Donna—the sister I may or may not reveal myself to and I wonder, but of course, I don't know and I doubt this sister of mine would know either, what it was like for my biological mother—our mother—as she had awaited my birth in a place far from home. Still, I try to imagine.

* * *

Denver, 1945

The months pass slowly for Grace. Her usually slim figure grows bulky with child. Instead of the glowing aura that surrounded her with her other pregnancies, she looks haggard.

I look so sad, she decides studying herself in the mirror. She gets out her compact and tries to cover the purple bruises under her eyes that have come with the endless tears. Blue eyes, blue woman; *maybe lipstick will help.* She puts on her brightest red lipstick. None of it helps. *Now I look like a sad clown.*

"You have to stop this crying," she commands her reflection in the mirror. "This baby will only know how to cry. It needs to know laughter, too."

But there was no laughter in her days of banishment.

Norton remains on base, avoiding her, condemning her by his absence.

The one thing keeping her going is imagining how surprised everyone will be when she arrives home, baby in arms. "Oh, the children are going to love having a little sister!"

When her labor starts the authorities at the home where she is living call Norton. He arrives at the hospital in time to name the child who will bear his name on her birth certificate but whose father he is not.

Through the fog of the anesthesia they have given her, she hears him say, "Grace, I am naming her Sharon Louise Bennod."

She knows Louise is the name of the woman he had planned to marry when he asked for a divorce. It is not the name she planned to give the baby if it was a girl but she's too groggy to argue. The nurse writes it on the birth certificate. The matter is settled.

When Sharon Louise is six weeks old Grace boards a train from Denver to travel to Erie, PA, baby in arms.

How passage for her and her tiny infant was secured remains a mystery to her. World War II is ending. All trains are "troop trains."

As she feared, the baby cries, drawing up her thin legs in pain. For six weeks she has tried to comfort her by offering another bottle of formula, thinking she must be hungry because she isn't gaining weight. She will never know her baby is actually allergic to milk fats. The only thing that comforts this poor baby is someone walking with her slung over their shoulder.

Grace has walked the train aisles for what feels like miles and she is exhausted.

A young soldier approaches her. He hardly looks old enough to be in uniform.

"Ma'am," he drawls hesitantly, "could I hold your baby for a while so you can get some sleep? My baby was born while I was in the fox holes of hell. I ain't never seen her. She's our first. I could practice by walking your baby in the aisles. I notice when you walk her, she gets quiet."

"I know I shouldn't hand her over to a stranger." After a brief pause Grace continued, "But you're in uniform. You must be a good man. And where would you go with her anyway?" Grace laughs tiredly, handing me over to first one soldier and then another throughout the long journey to Erie so she can eat or snatch a little sleep now and then.

(To this day the rhythm of train wheels riding the iron rails gives me soul-deep comfort and rest. And I have always loved men, especially men in uniform!)

When the train arrives at the station in Erie, Grace gets off carrying her six-week-old baby girl named Sharon, her own suitcase and a suitcase of beautiful baby clothes for her little one to wear when she is introduced to friends and family in Warren. She can't wait to introduce Donna and Norrie to their new baby sister. And how amazed her friends will be! Of course, there is bound to be some whispering. After all, Norton hadn't been home from the time he was drafted until he had come for her at Thanksgiving, but hopefully people will get bored counting and go on to another possible scandal.

No one has informed her that her baby will not be going home with her.

6

Gramma's House

Mom lied! She lied to me! How is it even possible? We have always been so close. I've been her companion in our life journey, forced to grow up at the age of seven.

Now I know she lied about what she knew about me. If she lied about that, what else has she lied about? Doesn't she trust my love for her? Doesn't she know that no other woman could ever replace her as my mother?

As it turns out, there are a lot of things that aren't quite as they seemed.

Now that the truth has begun to seep out, the crack in the dam opens wide and spills forth more and more truth about me, who I was and how I became who I am. It leaves me disoriented and afraid. I worry that I may never find myself again.

Even though I am angry and feeling betrayed, I can't deny how much I have been loved. I take comfort in remembering.

* * *

Daddy's father died before I was born but my delightful, Swedish grandmother, Emma, is very much alive and feisty. Daddy comes from a large family. One sister died of tuberculosis a few years before I was born but the others are living, most of them in or around Warren.

Aunt Evelyn, whom we call Auntie, was my Daddy's only unmarried sibling. She lives with Gramma at Gramma's house and works to earn a living for herself, Gramma and my Great-aunt Hilma.

Hilma has a big bump on her back and shuffles around all hunched over. She's always dressed in black dresses. She listens to the big radio that sits in the living room and when the announcer says, "Good Morning," Aunt Hilma always answers him. She smells old and she scares me just a little. Still, she has a big piggy bank on her bed that Auntie sometimes lets me hold and pet. I talk to it like Aunt Hilma talks to the radio, but I have to be very careful because it's breakable.

Gramma, Auntie, and Aunt Hilma live just four blocks from our house and we go there often.

Gramma speaks "Swenglish"—Swedish and English all mixed up together and sounding like a song. It isn't only the Italians who speak their language in their own houses. When the adults in Daddy's family want to say something they don't want us kids to understand, they speak Swedish.

Gramma has a big gas range in the kitchen that produces the best stuff in the world to eat. My favorite is a dish of warm rice with cinnamon or nutmeg on top and covered in thick cream. The grown-ups like her Swedish rye bread and the pies that she brings steaming hot to the table.

I sit for hours on the floor in the doorway between the kitchen and the dining room so I am not in the way, playing with her cooking pans, stirring a mix of buttons with a wooden spoon. The warmth of the kitchen, the spicy smell of nutmeg, the soft sounds of Swenglish cover me like a blanket. I feel warm and safe.

Gramma's back yard is like what I think heaven must be like. There is a weeping willow tree that has branches that touch the ground all around. I hide inside the leafy fort, imagining all sorts of secret things. My uncles are forever threatening to cut those blank-blank branches off. They tangle in the lawn mower and wind around their heads when they are trying to mow. But Gramma says, "No! The tree will keep *all* its branches. They belong to the *shildren*!" The branches stay.

Big, floppy grape leaves cover a grape arbor. Sometimes it will grow a few clusters of tiny sour grapes that nobody eats. It's my second favorite place because the real use of the grape arbor is not to produce grapes but to shade the long wooden picnic table underneath.

On Sunday afternoons in the summer, Gramma covers the table in a cheery blue and white checkered tablecloth and a whole bunch of family comes. The men are still wearing the suit pants they wore to church but not the jackets. They throw the jackets on the sofa in the house. Gramma tries to make them hang them up but no one does. The sleeves of their white shirts are rolled up nearly to their elbows, showing the muscles on their arms. They are working men. Their ties are loosened and the top buttons of their shirts undone. They endlessly tease Gramma, the kids, the aunts and each other.

The women are all dressed in neatly ironed cotton dresses that smell like starch and crinkle when they move. Gramma brings out a big pile of her aprons and tries to get them to put them on. "Save your clothes," she says crossly. But the pile of aprons lays untouched on the end of the long picnic table. The women hurry around bringing the food outdoors. We kids are rounded up and told to wash our hands under the outdoor spigot.

Everyone is laughing and eating thick sandwiches made of rye bread and cheese, with warm rice pudding for dessert. On the Fourth of July there is an icy cold watermelon. The juice drips down our chins and we spit seeds at one another. I am not a very good seed-spitter. Mine mostly land at my feet or stick on my clothes.

There used to be a fish pond in the yard but it's been filled with dirt. I am told that before I was born a little kid fell in and frightened everyone—especially the fish. I wish the pond was still there. I can imagine the golden fish swimming, hiding from the hot sun under lily pads.

There is also a vegetable garden and the patch of rhubarb. Everybody has those. Once when I was really little and Gramma was pulling rhubarb stalks to make a pie, I asked what it tasted like. She cut off a little piece and gave it to me. I shoved it in my mouth and bit down hard on it—-it drew all the spit right out of my mouth. I went howling to find Auntie! Gramma was howling too, with laughter. Aunt Evelyn gave her a bit of a scolding but her own face was rather puckered up and her body was shaking—I thought she was being *sympathetic* (that is my favorite new word. I like words). I was wrong.

Directly across the street from Gramma's house is a little family grocery store, Bovas' Market. When I was four the Bova family bought the house next to our house at the top of Russell Street. Their daughter Jill is just a year younger than me. We are *forever friends*.

Gramma's is a happy, safe place. I love going there.

My parents and I live in the house my mother's grandfather built years before. It's a three-story wooden house with a tin roof that sits at the very top of the hill—last house on the right on Russell Street: when it rains, the rain drums on the metal making a go-to-sleep sound. If you go way to the third floor and look out the window, you can see all the way to the Allegheny River.

Mom told me that my Great grandpa Peterson, who was from Sweden, built it as a boarding house so his wife, my Mom's grandma, and their daughters wouldn't have to work as house maids for other women in Warren. It was a success. Mom said her grandparent's family lived pretty good between the money from the boarders and the big garden they grew and the cow they had in the pasture up on the hill behind the house.

Later our house was made into apartments. Mom's mother, Clara, lived on the first floor. Uncle Jim and Aunt Margaret lived on the second floor. Great grandmother lived on the third floor and had a loom in the attic where she wove rugs until she was a really old lady and died. I went into the attic once. The loom was still up there. It was all apart and covered with cobwebs and dust. The attic was hot. I wondered how that old lady could stand weaving rugs up there in that hot dusty attic.

Mom said that when she and Daddy were married, Margaret and Jim bought a house on the next street over. Their back yards connected. After Great Grandmother died the second and third floors were opened to become one apartment where Mom and Daddy lived. When Mom's mother, Clara died, Mom and Dad borrowed enough money to buy out Uncle Jim's share of the house and they moved to the first floor and rented out the upstairs apartment to help pay the mortgage and taxes.

"That's how it was when you arrived, Becky," Mom told me.

I love this big old house because it has belonged to us forever. There is a front porch with furniture made of bent wood. It isn't very comfortable to sit on so Mom made some cushions and sewed bright orange covers for them. There is a hedge of orange blossoms that smell like perfume when they bloom. The flowers are actually white, they are called orange blossoms because they smell like warm oranges, sweet and juicy. There is a back porch with a porch swing just the right size for my Daddy and me to curl up on and swing on summer nights when the air is sweet with the smell of the orange blossoms riding on the breezes from the front yard and the sky is black velvet, all covered in stars. Sometimes Jill is allowed to come and sit with us—two little girls with a silly Daddy between us telling outrageous stories.

It's so safe and joyful. And it will only get better.

7

Mommy Won't You Buy A Baby

I t's 1948, I am three years old. Everyone wants to hear me talk because I use big words. My Daddy teaches me. People say I have an *amazing* vocabulary.

My Daddy found an RCA 78 record with a song I am sure is written just for me. It's called "Mommy Won't You Buy a Baby Brother (Or Sister) For Me"

Pretty soon I have it *memorized* and I sing it *continually*—with and without the record!

My favorite words are, "Mommy, won't you buy a baby brother or sister for me? Gosh, I'm awful lonely, bein' the only child–golly gee!"

I sing and sing and sing, begging for a brother or sister to play with.

Then in November, 1949, when I am four and a half years old, a beautiful, hazel-eyed, solemn six-month old baby boy is delivered right to our front door. The lady bringing him stomps the snow off her boots before coming in the house. She puts him into my mother's waiting arms. Daddy is standing with a big goofy grin on his face. My new brother is wrapped in a blue blanket. I am beside myself with joy. They *bought* me a baby brother, sure enough!

My parents name him James (after my mother's brother and the Bible James). We call him Jimmy. I adore him from the beginning but I am just a little *disappointed.* He rolls around and army-crawls across the floor but he's not as much of a playmate as I thought my brother would be.

Now our house is busy. Jimmy races around in a four-wheeled oblong metal cage the adults call a walker. That seems like a silly name to me. He isn't walking, he is rolling on wheels. The "walker" has a long handle that they attach sometimes and use to push it along like a buggy, but it's hard to steer so they hardly ever use the handle.

I heard Mom tell Aunt Margaret that the family that Jimmy used to belong to do not want my parents to adopt him. There's something about the way she said this. I know I am adopted. You are safe when you are adopted. Maybe Jimmy isn't really adopted. That worries me but I can't talk about it because I know I'm not supposed to be listening around the corner.

One day a lady who said she was his grandmother came to the house to visit him. She wanted to hold him but he screamed and buried his head in Mom's shoulder. I hope *she* never comes back. I heard Mom and Daddy talking in the kitchen later when they thought I was playing in the living room. Mom told Daddy a judge said that the grandmother couldn't ever come back. That makes me feel a little better but I can't ask about that either because then they would know that I am a "little pitcher with big ears." That's what they say if they are talking quietly and I come into the room. They look at me and say, "Little pitchers have big ears" —then they stop talking. I know they would be mad if they knew I had listened.

Mom tells me all the time, "I just love being a mommy!" I know she does because she laughs at us kids and hugs us a lot and she sings songs like "You Are My Sunshine" when she is dusting and cooking and taking care of us.

Daddy works at an auto-body shop removing dents and dings from cars and replacing destroyed parts. It's hard, dirty work and I heard Mom and Auntie say once that he is not a strong man. That's probably why he's so tired when he comes home from work.

When I was just a little kid, Mom and Daddy and I walked from where we live in the last house at the top of Russell Street to the bottom of Russell Street on Sunday mornings to get on the bus and go to church. We didn't have a car then. But before they *bought* Jimmy, Daddy bought a car. It's big and black and I love it. I sit in the back seat with my doll and we slide all over the back seat every time Daddy goes around a corner. I yell and Daddy laughs. Mom drives sometimes but I never slide when she's driving. She's very careful and kind of pokey.

When Daddy comes home from work and drives into the driveway, he slows down because there is a steep drop-off on the right side of the driveway and the house is on the left. The garage is all the way at the back of the house. The driveway scares Mom. She will go in but she never backs out. Daddy has to back the car out when Mom is going to drive.

Every time Daddy comes home, he yells, "How's my little family and my beautiful wife?" with a silly grin on his face but he always gets cleaned up before picking me up or pulling Mom into a bear hug and giving her a big noisy kiss that makes her laugh.

Except for when he first comes home from work, my Daddy always looks neat. "He looks like he just stepped out of a *bandbox*," I hear people say. I don't know what a *bandbox* is but it sounds like it is all clean and smells like soap. I think it must be a good place.

Mom gets upset when things don't go right. Aunt Polly, her best friend who lives in the house out back of us, tells her she can't be a mother and a *perfectionist*. Daddy almost never gets out of sorts. He just laughs and shrugs his shoulders and pats Mom on her butt which makes her yell, "Milton, the children!"

With our dark hair and our dark eyes, Jimmy and I favor him and if folks don't know we're adopted, they never think we are. But I know we're adopted. Mom and Daddy tell us all the time, "You are Mommy and Daddy's adopted darlings." We're special. It makes me feel proud.

One year after Jimmy's arrival, a six-day old baby girl is added to our family. They name her Deborah (after the Biblical judge). We call her Debbie.

We all have Bible names—Rebecca, James, and Deborah. I like that.

Debbie's a sweet baby, plump and smiley with blond hair and blue eyes, and soft skin the color of cream. She looks like Mom. People always say, "Debbie sure favors her mommy, and Becky and Jimmy are so much like you, Milton." And although I know that Jimmy and I come from different families, we look like "real" brother and sister.

Things sometimes get crazy in our household. Three kids. Two babies in diapers keep Mom really busy. She doesn't have as much time to play with me as she did before the little kids came. I am glad that when Daddy comes home from work, he still crawls around under the dining room table chasing me and making me scream until Mom says in her *I mean it voice*, "Milton! That's enough! She will never settle down to sleep tonight!"

Daddy gets up and throws up his hands yelling, "I surrender!" Then he puts his arms around her in a hug before he takes one of the babies to feed or change their stinky pants.

Sunday morning we used to always go to church together before we got the little kids. Daddy sang in the choir. Mom taught Sunday school. But, with the little kids, getting us all ready to go to church is just more than Mom can handle. She sends Daddy and me off to Sunday school and church on our own.

I love the Sundays when it is just the two of us. Daddy sings in the choir so he settles me in the second pew from the front of the church on the right—right in front of *the grandfathers.*

They are old men with whiskers and faded blue eyes that crinkle up when they smile. If they like what the preacher says they say "Amen" right out loud. I hear some of the other grown-ups try to shush them but they go ahead and do it anyway.

Once I'm all settled in my pew, I take out my doll, her blanket and a doll bottle from my purse and quietly play while church goes on around me.

When the choir has finished singing and just before the preacher starts to preach, Daddy comes down to sit with me. I leave my doll on her blanket on the bench and snuggle into his side. It is the best time of the week.

When we get home, the kitchen smells like roasted meat, mashed potatoes, cooked carrots, and coffee. We sit at the table and Daddy prays. The radio is on and the song "Showers of Blessing" always comes on just at the end of his prayer.

"We are showered with blessings" he says every Sunday and Mom agrees.

I will soon learn that showers sometimes turn into storms.

8

Gramma Falls Down

August 1951. I am six. Auntie Evelyn, Gramma, and I excitedly set off on a grand trip. We are going to take the train from Fredonia, NY to Rochester, NY to stay with my father's brother Carl, his only sibling who doesn't live in Warren, and with his family.

I vomit repeatedly from Warren to Fredonia—a relatively short trip. I dread the rest of the trip. At the train station Auntie buys me a package of crackers "to settle your tummy," but I have little faith in that remedy—it has never worked before, why should it now?

The train comes whistling and chuffing into the station. My heart beats hard in my chest in rhythm with its booming engine. We board. Auntie and Gramma make sure I have the window seat and we all press our foreheads against the window and wave good-bye. On the platform Mom and Daddy each hold a toddler. They all wave wildly until we can no longer see them.

For as long as I live, I will remember that picture of all of us.

As soon as the train is underway, I am no longer sick. I look at the package of crackers on the window ledge and know I won't need them. It is a miracle. I settle on the seat with my doll, watching the world go by. I sleep lulled by the rocking motion of the train, the click-clack song of its steel wheels singing along the track and by a sense of being at home in this place.

When we arrive in Rochester my Uncle Carl and Aunt Mary are there at the station to greet us with hugs and kisses.

Mom is a pretty lady with fine blond hair that she wears in a French twist. She always looks nice and smells good, but the only make-up she wears is a little pale pink lipstick. She doesn't wear nail-polish, she's too busy for that.

Aunt Mary has thick, black hair and red lipstick. Her finger nails shine with bright red nail polish and she just seems to bubble, like a pot of water on the stove when the heat is on high. She sweeps me into her arms and calls me "Honey Child." The fragrance of her perfume clings to me like love with a smell.

Uncle Carl is an accountant. He is the branch manager of Ernst and Ernst. Auntie says that's a *national accounting firm* but I'm not sure what that is. He is the most *prosperous* (this is another word I like—it sounds rich) one in my father's family. Their house has a patio! I know that only rich houses have patios—and they have a den and a big living room and dining room and a *foyer* (that's a word they just taught me). I would call it a big hallway. I wonder if I will get lost in this big house and I am just a little afraid.

Before dinner, they serve Auntie and Gramma cocktails—no one I know has cocktails but I do know they have alcohol in them and I am a little shocked. But they are laughing and having so much fun, I decide it's OK.

My boy cousins are older than I. Carl is 19. He's the oldest. Then comes Dave, Tom, and finally there is Mary Anne, who is a year younger than I am. They don't seem too happy to have a little cousin they are supposed to play with. Mary Ann pouts, but mostly the cousins ignore me except for Carl. He seems to know I feel lonely and he fusses over me. I fall in love with him and decide I will love him best of all of them forever.

When we have been here a few days, Auntie and Grandma decide to go shopping in the city, see the big department stores; have lunch at one of them.

"We will be *elegant ladies* and you will come with us and be an *elegant lady*, too, Becky," they declare.

We climb onto the city bus to ride downtown. It is just the three of us *elegant ladies* out on the town. We marvel at the displays in the huge department store windows, oohing and aahing over such luxury.

Suddenly, Gramma falls down on the sidewalk and is vomiting. There is a lot of commotion. An ambulance comes and takes Gramma and Auntie away. I am left in the care of a clerk at the department store until my Uncle Carl and Aunt Mary are called. Someone comes to get me and takes me back to the house.

The next day Daddy arrives. He has driven from Warren to get me and to see Gramma who is in the hospital. I hear the grown-ups talking in hushed voices. They say Gramma has had a serious heart attack. I am not sure what that means but I can tell it is something very scary.

Daddy drives me home. I vomit most of the way.

Gramma dies in the hospital in Rochester on August 27, 1951. Her body is shipped home and taken to the *funeral home.* I don't like the funeral home. It is not a home at all. There are flowers everywhere and they don't smell sweet like the flowers outdoors. The smell of them makes my head spin and my stomach feel sick. It is the last place I see Gramma.

Now Auntie has to move out of the house where she and Gramma lived for so many years, the one across the street from Bova's Market, because the house doesn't belong to them. It was theirs to live in as long as my grandparents were alive. My grandfather Samuelson, Daddy's dad, used to work for a wealthy woman who let them live in the house as part of his pay but now that Gramma's dead, the house has *reverted to the woman's estate* (that's what I hear the grown-ups say) and Auntie is homeless.

Fortunately, Auntie is a music teacher. She has been teaching for the past few years with an elderly woman who lives alone in a big house on Pennsylvania Avenue, Mrs. Russell. Mrs. Russell's *late husband—* that's what they say when you are dead—you are *late:* I guess you must always be late—because you can't get there on time when you are dead. In fact, you can't get there at all. Anyway Mr. Russell was a doctor. Auntie told me Mrs. Russell and the late Doctor Russell used to travel around the world in their younger days and that the *furnishings of the house reflect their travels.*

Now the house's white paint is peeling off in places making it look sad. After the doctor died Mrs. Russell didn't have much money so she teaches piano students to make some. The house costs a lot to heat, Auntie says, and taxes are high and Mrs. Russell is lonely in that big rambling place.

Just like our house, the second floor was been made into an apartment, so Mrs. Russell gets some rent money to help her out but it's not enough. That's why Mrs. Russell invited Auntie to come and live with her. They could both teach and put their money together and Mrs. Russell wouldn't be so lonely anymore. Auntie says it her only *option.*

No matter what time of year it is there is always the smell of gas in the house. It makes me feel a little dizzy when I first go in there.

"It's from the pilot lights on the gas range and from the space heaters in the winter," Auntie says, "but it is cozy," she adds like she doesn't quite believe it.

Mrs. Russell is old and she always feels chilly, so the living room and the *studio,* that's what they call the music room, and their bedroom just off the studio are always warm and stuffy with the smell of gas and *lavender* perfume and of old lady clothes with fur and lace.

The studio was once the formal living room. There are two nine-foot Steinway pianos that sit side by side in the front part. Behind the pianos there is a space for what they call the classroom where we students—the willing and the unwilling, of which I am one of the unwilling—sit on cold metal chairs and learn *music theory* from work books. We have to fill in the names of notes and scales played on the piano, and we have to learn stuff from dusty chalk words and notes on a blackboard.

Music theory is a terrifying mystery to me and I sit trembling with fear that I will be called on to give an answer to a question I don't even understand.

I don't like the studio. I don't even like to walk through it but I have to. I don't know yet but the music lessons will go on for years; years of never quite understanding, never quite getting my fingers to obey the notes my eyes see on paper but my mind won't grasp. Right now, all I know is I hate music lessons!

The only thing worse than music theory is "The Recital."

We students are paraded before an audience of parents and friends. They never look very happy to be there. They don't look very friendly to me. They look at us with eyes that are dark and judging to see if their child is the best player or if we are any better this year then we were last year.

My heart bangs in my chest, a wild thing trying to get out. I can hardly breathe. I have practiced and practiced my piece. I can play it perfectly at home, even without the music, but when I sit down on the bench at "The Recital" all the notes seem to fly out of my head. But year after year my fingers get me through without doing anything too shameful.

When there are no lessons going on and no recitals, Mrs. Russell's is a fun place to visit. Sometimes my brother and sister and I stay overnight, sharing the old red pull out couch in the living room.

Everything in Mrs. Russell's house is red—red oriental carpets, red glass on the mantel, red roses in vases in the summertime. Even Mrs. Russell's cheeks have patches of red rouge just below her still bright blue eyes.

While the living room, studio, and bedroom are warm in the wintertime because of the gas space heaters, the kitchen at the back of the house is so cold we sometimes put on our coats to go back there. It seems to me we only eat soup and sandwiches so we don't have to spend much time in the kitchen getting it ready but Mom says maybe it's all they can afford to eat. Mom always sends some leftovers home with Auntie when she comes to see us.

Auntie moved in with Mrs. Russell a few months after Gramma died. The house on Canton Street was sold to strangers. The *enchanted* yard is no longer ours to play in or even to visit. When I go with Jill to her parents' store across the street from Gramma's old house, I look longingly, wishing I could go back.

9

We All Fall Down

It is March of 1952. Although Gramma is gone and Auntie has moved, life goes on. The snows of winter finally melt and there is talk in our house of what seeds to buy for the garden in the coming summer.

Jimmy, "Mr. Sober-sides" we call him because he always looks so serious, is growing. He will be three in May and is turning into the playmate I visualized way back when I sang "Mommy Won't You Buy a Baby Brother (or Sister) For Me."

Debbie, chubby and charming at 18 months, is the one now in the walker and rolling all over the house. Although Jimmy and I both walked by the time we were a year old, Debbie has decided that balancing on her feet and walking is just too much trouble, so instead she tears around in the old metal walker.

Jimmy's adoption is *still not finalized*. I hear my parents talking about it when they don't think I am listening, *but it is getting closer*. Debbie and I are firmly in the family with all the necessary documents to prove it.

Daddy tells Mom, "None of that stuff matters because we are a family and we love one another to death."

By now we are all going to church together. Mom and Daddy talk to Jesus as if He lives right in our house with us even though we can't see Him. I like that.

March is birthday month for both my Daddy and me. His is March 7th, mine the 30th. He will be 42 and I will be 7—what a month! He is much more excited about my coming birthday than about his own.

"Magillicuddy," he says—Magillicuddy is his pet name for me. "You will be so surprised when you get your birthday present! Let's see...how many more days?"

I am so excited that the days seem to go by like a snail crawling on the sidewalk after a rain. I think it will never get to be the 30th.

Daddy sells Bibles. He is a fairly new Christian and is very excited about Jesus and the Bible. Because he is so happy when he goes to people's houses to sell them Bibles and because he always looks like he just stepped out of his bandbox, he sells lots of Bibles.

For the past four months Daddy had been seeing a doctor because of *a heart condition*, I hear Mom tell Aunt Polly. She says that when he was just a little kid, he had *rheumatic fever* and it left his heart damaged.

"But he is doing well," Mom tells Aunt Polly when she sees I am in the kitchen. "We aren't worried at all."

But now he has pneumonia—*double pneumonia*, I hear them whisper ominously.

Mom is not home. No one tells me why but I listen when no one thinks I am around. I learn Daddy is terribly sick. He is in the hospital. Mom only comes home to change clothes once in a while. Aunt Polly comes to take care of us during the day. Auntie comes after work and spends the nights. Aunt Margaret and Uncle Jim can't help because they are living in Cleveland.

Church folks drop off food and tell me not to worry—they are praying. Friends and neighbors do whatever they can. Daddy rallies. Everyone gives a sigh of relief but no one is terribly surprised. After all, everyone has been praying hard for him.

Maybe Daddy will come home tomorrow. After all, tomorrow is Sunday—God's special day. Mom comes home to rest and to spend time with us and for the first time in days, I relax. I didn't realize I had been living while holding my breath but now I can breathe. I hug her, not wanting to let go.

Jimmy clings to her, holding onto the hem of her dress everywhere she goes. Debbie sobs out her relief in Mom's arms until her sobs end in little hic-ups.

The sun shines once again at our house. Monday will be a good day in school, I know.

Sometime in the night, the phone rings and someone at the hospital tells Mom Milton is *failing*. Mom calls Aunt Polly. She comes to spend the night at the house with us while her husband, Uncle Hap, takes Mom back to the hospital.

In the morning, Mom comes home. Her face is gray and saggy. Her eyes look like dark holes that are so deep they go all the way down to her heart. She goes right into her bedroom and quietly shuts the door. I hear her crying. It sounds funny, like she has buried her face deep into a pillow.

I don't know what's wrong with my Mom until Aunt Polly takes me aside and says in her *brave voice*, "Your Daddy went to be with Jesus last night. Just think, Becky, instead of being at Bethlehem Covenant Church, singing in the choir, he is singing with the heavenly choir in the presence of his Lord."

Maybe Daddy is singing in heaven but I want him here with me on earth. Someone takes the little kids but I'm allowed to stay with Mom. People come but no one knows what to say. It seems that all around me there is only stunned silence broken by quiet sobbing.

Daddy died at 6:52 AM, Sunday, March 16th, nine days after his birthday and two weeks before mine.

(Mom told me years later she thought she would just die of grief and fright. She had never even backed the car out of the garage, much less out of that horrible driveway. Daddy had not been able to get insurance on the mortgage nor on the car loan because of his heart. He only had a small life insurance policy that barely paid for his funeral. She had no idea how she could ever keep us together and alive.)

This is second funeral in my young life. I don't remember the funeral itself but I remember being at the funeral home for long hours of *visitation*. I clutch my doll, kneeling quietly by one of the upholstered chairs near the coffin. People coming to *the visitation* all have thoughts and opinions that gush out of their open mouths, their teeth and lips come unhinged and let every thought inside their heads come out. They drown me with their stupid words.

"It is so shocking," I hear over and over.

But the most frightening words I hear are, "Will you keep the children? Maybe you should just keep the girls. It's hard for a single woman to raise a son."

My world is shattering and I can do nothing to stop it. I can't stop the words. I can't stop people I love from dying but I *must not cry* so my Mom will feel better.

After patting Mom's hands and talking in their stupid voices they come swooping like vultures, all in black, to where I am quietly playing and pat me on the head informing me, "You are your mother's big helper now."

I take that advice very seriously and after those two days at the funeral home, I am no longer a little girl. I have been launched into a realm of responsibility far beyond my not quite seven years of age.

When Mom cries, I comfort her, reassuring her, "Daddy is in heaven with Jesus now. It will be OK," convincing neither of us but valiantly trying to be the "big girl" and become my mother's companion. It will be my role for the rest of our lives together.

(Many years later, when I became a pastor and was officiating a funeral of a father who also left a little girl behind, I took the child by the hand and we went to a quiet place where I reassured her that although her daddy was dead, she was still a little girl, she was not expected to take care of her mother, her mother would take care of her. She sobbed with relief into my shoulder.)

Two weeks after Daddy died, Mom gives me my birthday present—the one he was so excited about. It is wrapped in paper with puppies and hearts all over it. I open it carefully, fearing I might tear the paper my Daddy wrapped around my gift. There inside is a Bible. The cover is black leather, it has a zipper that goes around three sides and on the front in gold letters is my name, Rebecca Samuelson.

Because I was going to be a big girl of seven and was learning to read in first grade, he had ordered a Bible especially for me. He couldn't wait to see my face when I opened it. I lifted it up to heaven and thanked him. I took it into my bed at night. I opened the zipper carefully and looked at the words I had not yet learned to read. I traced my finger over the gold letters with my name and I cried with my face buried deep in my pillow so Mom wouldn't hear me and be sad.

A few weeks after the funeral, more terrifying trouble arrives.

We three kids are stricken with measles. A quarantine sign is nailed to the house. These are *Nine-day Measles,* the kind that can leave a child blind, or brain damaged, or even dead. For days and nights on end my mother nurses her children, as one after another we fall victim to high fevers and delirium.

(Years later Mom told me, "When it was all over and each of you was not only alive but well, I knew without a doubt, I could handle anything—we would make it.")

We recover. Mom learns to back the car out of the garage and driveway. She applies for government surplus food so we always have dried milk, the thought of which make me gag to this day. There is oleo margarine with a little red spot that I get to knead into the pale fat to make it look like butter. We also get yellow cheese and flour. With these ingredients in hand, even if we are sometimes low on meat, we always have fresh yeast rolls and cheese served with a cool, jiggling red *Jell-O* to feast on and nasty milk to drink.

I miss my Daddy terribly but never more so than after I go to bed at night.

When I was little, Daddy would always come in and fluff my pillow before I went to sleep, turning the cool side up. When he would leave the room, I would turn it back to the warm side. Now that he is gone, I lie in bed, clutching my Bible, feeling guilty—hating it that I ever turned my pillow and undid what he had done for me.

The folks who rent the apartment upstairs become Mom's dear friends and life-line in many ways; not only financial but emotional and social. Lucille, the lady, and her husband, Earl, have one child, a little girl, Sharon. She is impossibly spoiled. I envy her. We join families and foods for dinner several times a week. We are finding a new way to live.

Many of Mom's friends come and go—at least at first. And it seems most of their husbands are only too happy to lend a hand to the pretty young widow in distress. This has made *tension* in several homes! Mom knows but there is nothing she can do about it. She needs help with fixing things around that big old house and on the aged, not quite reliable car. She certainly can't afford to pay someone to do the work. Some people accuse her of being snobby: *acting above her station* or even trying to get the other women's husbands. It seems as long as women see her as poor and helpless, in need of charity, it is fine. But once she learns to hold her head up and take care of herself, her children, and her home, she is fair game for *criticism* and even some *malicious* gossip. Slowly but surely, she develops a shell of self-defense.

But it isn't over yet.

10

Learning To Go On

On September 19, 1952, six months after Daddy died and just a little over one year since our fateful visit to Rochester with Gramma's death and my little girl love affair with my kindly cousin Carl, we receive more bad news. Young Carl had gone to work in the morning, had come home in the late afternoon not feeling well and within hours was dead. He had died of Bulbar Polio, a fast-moving killer.

Then there was the matter of Jimmy's adoption. He wasn't adopted. There had been no chance to finalize the adoption before Daddy's death.

Many of Mom's friends, even Aunt Margaret and Uncle Jim, told her she should, "Send Jimmy back!" This was said in voices low and clinically practical.

"I have already lost my husband, I *will not* give up my son as well," Mom retorted angrily.

("Your mother put Uncle Jim and me to shame that day," Aunt Margaret told me recently. "I would have given anything to be able to take back those words but they had been spoken. We weren't being helpful. We'd only put a knife in her heart. For a long, lonely time afterward there was a chasm between us.")

Mom may have looked meek and mild but where her children were concerned, she was a fighter. She petitioned the court to be allowed to adopt Jimmy but was told a single parent could not adopt. I have no idea who the person was who arranged and financed her battle, but battle she did. She collected letters from some very prominent people testifying to her character and her ability to take care of all three of her children. On the day the court was to rule, Mom and Jimmy, who was now 5, went together to the courthouse.

When they returned home, my sober little brother came flying up the steps to the front porch yelling at the top of his lungs, "I'm adopted to my mother! I'm adopted to my mother!"

I wonder if anyone had realized how frightened he had been, or how much he had sensed the weight of the pending decision. From that day to this, he was our mother's child. He never needed, or even wanted, to know about his family of origin—he had all he needed in Mom.

I, on the other hand, wanted to know more about myself, about my origins. Whenever I'd ask Mom, her answer was the same.

"How would I know? You were born in Denver, CO. I would have no idea."

I continued to insist I was a twin.

"Rebecca! You are not a twin. Your birth certificate clearly states you were a single birth. Don't be silly," she announced in her *and this is the end of the conversation* voice.

I knew better than to press the subject but I felt some critical part of me was missing.

Over the years, no matter how I would try to broach the subject with her, her answer never changed by so much as a word, "How would I know? You were born in Denver, CO," until the day she let slip, "and you were brought to Erie by train."

Once, as a young mother myself, I thought I could "guilt" her into telling me more.

"Mom, I really need to know my family medical history. Surely you know something."

But she would not be forced, even by guilt, to reveal the deep, dark secret of my beginnings.

It wasn't easy for Mom to raise us alone. While the "little kids" were still too young to go to school, Mom was determined to stay at home and provide a stable home for us. She made shell jewelry and sold it to her friends and their friends. She was artistic and the necklaces and earrings were beautiful. They didn't buy them out of pity. They bought them because they were lovely and they were *the thing* to have in the 1950s.

Mom worked as an answering service for an Electrolux salesman who came by the house to pick up his messages rather than call for them, never missing a chance to visit the pretty young widow.

She could pinch a penny until it bled a dollar.

And people were unbelievably kind.

That hair, that baby fine hair of Mom's was a constant trial to her. Keeping her coiffure was second only to God and caring for her children. Much to her despair, she could no longer afford to have her hair done at the beauty salon every week—or even at all.

There was a salon at the foot of Russell street. The owner, Angie, had a soft heart and a young man stylist, Phil, who needed the practice on "up-dos." Angie would have my mother wash her own hair at home, then bring her rollers with her and come to the salon. Phil would set her hair in rollers. She'd don a scarf and drive home. When her hair was dry, she'd return and Phil would take out the rollers, teasing the reluctant strands into fullness, twisting and spraying them until they became a French twist with a few curls to frame her face.

The twist was further lacquered until it became a nearly impermeable helmet which she protected each night by wrapping it in yards of carefully preserved toilet paper, all held in place by a pink satin nightcap which allowed her to turn over at night with a gliding, sliding motion.

If she was forced to go out in wind or rain, there was the trusty plastic rain bonnet sans any fashion to protect her hair. "Never mind, I'll look good when I get there," she'd say to me if I suggested maybe it wasn't such a lovely thing. But then, nearly everyone else's mother wore one, so I guess it was ok.

(Phil eventually bought the beauty shop, renamed it Phillip's and moved it to Conewango Ave. When at the age of 34, I became a beautician, it was

Phil who hired me and patiently taught me what can't be learned in beauty school. I, however, never did master the art of the up-do!)

It wasn't only the beauty shop owner who had compassion for my mother. The owner of Lewis's meat market did as well.

Mom shopped very carefully, adding up every penny as she put only necessary items in the cart.

I will never forget, I was with her that first shopping trip after Dad's death—in fact, I was usually with her. I remember how worried she was about spending the money necessary to feed us. The food friends and neighbors had brought us was gone. The cupboards and refrigerator were pretty bare. The cart was terrifyingly full. The store's owner, Mr. Lewis, was at the register. As he rang up the groceries, he packed them, bag after bag while Mom watched in resignation knowing that her money would soon be gone. As he packed the last bag, he turned to Mom, smiled sweetly and said, "That will be five dollars, please."

"Five dollars! My goodness, that isn't right. I owe you a lot more that that!"

"No, Dorothy," he said, "That will be five dollars."

In his own time and in his own way, God unfailingly provided for us but I didn't always appreciate that.

At the time it seemed to me that my whole life was difficult and unfair: unfair that I missed out on being a child because I had to care for my siblings, unfair that my daddy had died so young, unfair that we had to scrimp and scratch for every penny; yet it never occurred to me to be mad at God or even to wonder if I might be better off in my *real* family. I just wanted to *know more about me*—and of course, to find my twin.

11

Are You Sure?

I n just a few more minutes I will reach the inglorious place where I am supposed
to meet Donna. What sort of Pandora's Box will I open if I tell her who I am,
that I am her sister?

The days and weeks following Aunt Margaret's revelation come roaring
back into my memory.

* * *

The information Aunt Margaret has given me is as not something I can share
with anyone who lives in Warren. It's a small town where everyone knows
everyone, and if they don't know someone, they are sure to know someone
who does. Gossip is its great past-time.

Yet, I have to talk about this with someone besides just Jon and my aunt.
After some internal debate I decide to share with my close friend/double
cousin Joyce. Joyce grew up in Warren—we went to church together, we
shared classes in school. I often times stayed at her house when we were
young. Now she is living in Columbus, Ohio. I feel that's far enough away
and I know she doesn't have a close relationship with many people in Warren
after all these years and she can be trusted with my secret.

I pick up the phone and call her. After some informal chit-chat I say in the most casual voice I can master, "Joyce, I have found my birth family. I want to share with you but you have to *promise* not to tell anyone else!"

"I promise but Becky, who is it? Is it someone from Warren?"

"My mother is Grace Bennod; her husband is Norton."

There is a long, heavily laden silence on the other end of the line and then she utters three small words that will stay with me forever.

"Are you sure?"

The tone of her voice immediately makes me defensive. I'm not absolutely sure. I only have my Aunt Margaret's long buried memory and a picture of a brother who once looked just like our son for proof. But that tone makes me feel both threatened and angry for reasons I can't understand.

"Of course, I am sure!" I reply indignantly.

Hesitantly she goes on, "Becky, I knew your family. Our backyards met at the bottom of that little hill out back of our house. You have a sister who is two years younger than we are. Her name is Virginia and if you look in our yearbook you will find her picture. She and I used to play together when we were very young. Once we took my red wagon and went around collecting those old glass soda bottles that had a refund. We dragged them to the grocery store to turn them in for cash. I think we probably bought candy with the money! I can't imagine what else we would have done with it. I remember your family but my memories are a child's memories and I won't share them with you because they would be skewed." She speaks as though she is weighing, measuring, every word she is saying.

"I will look in the yearbook. Thanks," I say abruptly. There is nothing else to be said except "Good bye."

I get out my yearbook and find my younger sister. I flip to my senior picture, then her sophomore picture and then back to my picture. We could be twins if she hadn't been wearing *cat-eye* glasses. I wore glasses in high school, too, but didn't wear them for my senior picture. *More proof.* Still, Joyce's silence and her question, "Are you sure?" weigh heavily on me.

About a week later, as I am driving my step-father to Erie to visit with Mom in the rehab, I decide to share my secret with just one more person, Dad. I have called my step-father, Dave Titus, Dad for years now. I resisted for a long time. I remembered my Daddy, but Jimmy and Debbie didn't remember him so they called Dave "Dad" right from the start. Eventually, his persistent love won me over. There is no question in my mind he can be trusted with this secret and somehow it just seems right to share it with him.

"Dad, I have learned who my biological family is," I say as casually as I can, not looking at him, keeping my hands on the wheel, eyes on the road.

"Oh, you have? And who is it?" he asks. He doesn't sound surprised but as a law officer, a retired game warden, he knows how to keep his expressions neutral.

"My mother's name is Grace Bennod and her husband is Norton," I tell him, glad to unburden myself just this one more time.

He is quiet for some time, seemingly trying to make a decision. Dad is never one to act without carefully assessing a situation. Finally, he begins to talk. He doesn't turn his head to address me, he speaks to the windshield in a distant voice.

"That's right, Becky. One time I was called to do an investigation into a deer that had been taken illegally. It was at the Bennod house. They were just cutting it up when I came and didn't try to deny they had taken it. They hadn't shot it. It was a fresh road-kill and in those days a citizen couldn't take it, only a law officer could and the meat had to go to the county home. The laws have changed and now a citizen can take fresh road kill. I really think they needed the meat and I felt bad but I had to fine them. I gave them the lowest fine I could. They paid the fine and turned the meat over without any fuss."

He continued, "When I got home, your mom asked me, 'Did you see the wife? Was she there?' It was an odd question for her to ask. She had never asked about a woman present in any house before and she seemed fussed or threatened or something. I told her that there was a wife there, but that I didn't pay much attention and wanted to know why she was asking me that. 'Because that is Becky's mother,' your mom said. "Becky who?" I asked her, totally puzzled. 'Our Becky,' she said angrily, 'and I don't ever want to hear or talk about any of this again. And you will never tell anyone!' I was so stunned that I couldn't think of a single thing to say. I think it is the only time in my life I just stood with my mouth open, speechless."

Now *I* am too stunned to speak. My driving goes on autopilot as my mind tries to cope with this stunning revelation. *Here is the proof! Now there is no question, no more wondering. This is from the mouth of my own mother coming now that she is no longer able to utter an intelligible word. And she knew! She knew all along and she lied to me!*

My emotions swing wildly between elation, fear, betrayal and rage, but it is the rage that frightens me the most.

Did Mom not trust my love enough to share this with me? Did she think I would transfer my loyalty to another woman and not love her anymore? Didn't she know how powerful my love is for her?

In my mind there is no other reason possible for her to have kept this from me for 44 years other than that she feared I would transfer my love to my biological mother. I am devastated by the thought.

After a while I calm down and ask Dad a few questions, but when we arrive at the rehab and I see my mother a wave of rage washes over me nearly knocking me down, drowning me. It's hard for me even to say anything much less give her my usual kiss. I am grieving. I just don't know this is grief—the anger phase of grief.

The parts of my story that I know now, nag at me, invading my every waking moment and slithering into my dreams at night. It is so much—it is so little.

Some months later, Joyce comes to Warren to visit her parents and stay with them for a few days.

Her mother, Martha, still wears house dresses with a full apron over to keep them clean, just as she did when we were kids. She has aged since the days I came to stay overnight and play with Joyce by the hour, but she still has deep dimples when she smiles and she is a chronicler of lives. She cuts out notices from the newspaper of births, deaths, and achievements of everyone she ever knew and pastes them into her books—the books of life.

After being shooed out of the kitchen by her mother who is preparing dinner, Joyce heads to the living room and sits in her mother's chair, fitting her own body into the indentations left by her mothers' body, surprised she has grown to fit them.

Beside her mother's chair, Joyce finds a stack of newspapers waiting to be cut apart and pasted into the appropriate books. She picks up the newspaper on the top of the pile assuming it is the current edition of the Warren news. When she opens it to check out the obituaries, the place we usually begin reading in our now adult lives, she finds the obituary for Grace Bennod.

Looking around to be sure her mother and brother are far enough away they can't hear her, she picks up the phone and calls me.

"Becky, did you know Grace Bennod just died? Her obituary is in the paper," she whispers into the phone in haste. "I can't talk. I don't want my family to hear me but you can look it up."

"It can't be!" I cry out. "I would have seen it. I've known my mother's name for months now and I always read the obituaries. I couldn't have missed it!"

"Well, I'll go check the date and call you back when I can, but I just read it," she whispers and quickly hangs up the phone.

After supper, she calls again. "The date of her death was March 15," she informs me.

It is now the end of March. Our old newspapers have gone into the trash. But, just in case, I scrabble through the stack on the closet shelf, the stack awaiting garbage day. I look and look checking dates over and over until my fingers are black with newspaper ink but I have no paper with Grace's obituary.

"I've got to go the library and check there," I tell Jon after filling him in on Joyce's call. He sighs, knowing there will be no dissuading me.

"You are too emotional to drive safely. I'll take you," he announces firmly. We bundle up against the late winter ice and snow and he drives to the library. It is closed.

The next day we are at the library as soon as it opens. He has become as anxious as I am. We head for the newspapers. The copies of the Warren papers don't go back more than a few days, so I seek the help of staff to obtain papers going back to the 15th. They bring them to us and both Jon and I eagerly go through them. There is no obituary for Grace Bennod.

We go home and I call Joyce, praying she'll be the one to answer the phone. She is.

"Joyce, you have to look at that paper again! We went to the library and there is no obituary."

"I will when I can. I'll call you back," she whispers. I can tell she is as puzzled as I am.

It's only a matter of minutes before the phone rings again.

"You won't believe this, Becky, but that paper is a year old. Your mother died a year ago, March 15, 1989!"

My first thought on hearing her words is, *Oh, no! What if I did her hair and didn't know it was my mother. I don't think I could bear that.*

A few years ago, I had worked at Phillip's Beauty Shop—the same Phillip who had done my mother's hair so long ago. After I stopped working in the shop, I began to work with one of the local funeral directors, Mark Patterson, doing women's hair. To me it is a ministry. Each time I style a deceased woman's hair, I pray for the loved ones who are left behind and who have to go on living in this person's absence. But what if one of those women was my mother, was Grace? I can't remember the names of all the women I have prepared for viewing. I *have to* find that obituary and see if Mark Patterson did her funeral. I shudder deep within to think I may have come that close to seeing my birth mother and never knew it.

With heavy heart and trembling limbs, we get into the car and once again Jon and I set off for the library. This time we go into the archives on microfilm. And there I find the obituary.

Someone makes a copy for me. I decide to wait until we are home to read it. The question; *Who am I?*, is coming closer to having an answer. The closer it comes, the more frightened I become of what I'll find.

At home, I study the obituary, pouring over every word. I learn I not only have an older brother Norton Jr. and an older sister Donna and a younger sister Virginia, but also a younger brother David. For some reason, that surprises me.

The obituary states that my older brother and his wife live in Florida. Donna and her husband live in nearby Russell, PA, Virginia and her husband live in Lexington, KY and my younger brother lives at home. I wonder why a man his age is still living at home. Is there something wrong with him?

Finally, I get to the bottom of the article and find that Grace had not been at Mark Patterson funeral home. I cry with relief.

Then, like a bolt of unexpected lightening zipping through blue sky, the thought strikes me; *I've lost both my mothers*. Grace died as Dorothy was in a deep coma and since she came out of the coma, she has never been able to walk or talk. They are both gone, each in her own way.

I sob, this time in grief.

Now that I know the names of my half-siblings, I begin to watch the newspaper for any mention of them. One day I read that my older sister Donna is membership chairman of the Warren Art League. The Art League is holding a show on the court house lawn the next week. It is too much of an opportunity to pass up. Perhaps I can at least get a look at her. Maybe even say a few words, although I have no idea what words.

One thing I do know, I am not in the least bit artistically gifted.

Several years ago, Auntie and I took an art appreciation course at a local college. For one lesson we were given the assignment to create an abstract painting. I labored creating *abstract sunflowers*. Thankfully, we didn't have to sign our works but the professor did collect them. Taking them one by one, he commented on each one. When he got to mine, he said, "And here we have someone who must have been feeling hungry—they painted bananas and fried eggs!"

Most assuredly, I won't be joining the Art League.

The day of the Art League Show dawns warm and sunny. Sunny, warm Saturdays are rare in Warren, so there is a festive air about the Art Show.

I talk our youngest into going with me. Barb and I wander by tables with women seated on chairs looking official but talking among themselves, apparently not a bit interested in anyone who might be approaching with an inquiry or desire to sign up for their club.

(It shames me now to remember how I looked them over, one by one, and decided I wouldn't want a single one of them to be my sister. They were too fat, or too old, or too unkempt, or too snooty, not at all what I had in mind to call family.)

We walk on. Eventually we come upon an artist I know and I ask her if she knows Donna and if she is present. Her voice is snotty as she tilts her head back to observe me and looks down her aristocratic nose to address me. "No. Donna is NOT here."

Barb and I look at one another. What the heck was that all about?

Without looking at a single painting, Barb and I leave.

Barb looks at me with worry in her eyes. "Mom, let's go to the Plaza and steady ourselves with a big piece of coconut meringue pie each and cups of strong, scalding hot black coffee. There is nothing like caffeine and sugar to help one recover from shock!"

I vow right here and now that I will never go looking for my siblings again. If God wants me to find them, he will have to do the job himself because I'm not up to any more of this emotional chaos.

In fact, I'm an emotional wreck. Every time I try to talk about anything related to my biological family, I cry.

Soon, I'm crying over just about everything related to anything. It's becoming harder and harder for me to go see Mom in the nursing home. Grief and resentment are taking over my life. Knowing I can't go on this way, I beg Jon to find me a counselor.

I can't even do the research to locate one myself. He arranges for me to see a Christian counselor and he drives me there. I cry the whole first session. But my healing is beginning.

The counselor tells me fear is common among parents who adopt. There is always the possibility, in their minds, that the birth parents might show up and demand to have their child returned.

"Even though all the legal papers are in order," she says, "they fear losing their children, and that fear becomes so deeply seated that it carries over long past the time the children have become adults."

This is something I never considered but after thinking about it, I realize it makes a lot of sense. I realize Mom was not only an adopting mother but a single mother, as well, in an era when someone might possibly challenge her right to keep us. I remember her battle to legally adopt Jimmy and realize how that might have affected her sense of security for the rest of her days. But I am still angry.

At another session, the counselor asks me why, when I have known I was adopted since I was very young, I have never gone searching for my biological family. I answer without hesitation, "I always said if God wants me to meet my family, He will bring them to me in *His* time."

"What has changed?" she asks.

I consider her question for some time before answering, "Nothing, I guess."

"Then I suggest you write on a 3x5 card; *I will wait for the Lord,* and carry it with you at all times. When you feel anxious, take it out and look at it. Remind yourself, He is in charge."

As I work with first one counselor and then another, I begin to find a degree of healing. It is easier to visit Mom in the nursing home. My words become more loving and gentle and at times even joy-filled.

We sing Sunday school songs and while she can't speak words, she sings, "Jesus love me this I know, for the Bible tells me so. Little ones to Him belong. They are weak but He is strong. Yes, Jesus loves me. Yes, Jesus loves me. Yes, Jesus loves me. The Bible tells me so." She sings every word without faltering.

We hug and we kiss once again.

On September 20, 1992, Dad and I visit Mom in the afternoon. It has been a good visit. As I say goodbye, she takes my face in her hands and speaks clearly, "I love you."

"Oh, Mom, I love you, too!"

Later that night, Jon and I get a call from Dad.

"The Rouse Home just called. Your mom died in her sleep this evening. When they went in to do a bed check at 9 PM, she was gone," he tells us.

In the weeks to come, we are told that for several days Mom had been refusing her medications. I think she understood that the blood thinners were keeping her alive and she had lived as long as she felt the Lord expected her to. She had given all she could. She had given herself first for her children and then her husband, trying to keep us all alive, healthy and safe. Now it was her turn to be totally healed and at home in the safety of her Father's House where there are many rooms.

I realize that now both my mothers have died, God has opened the door for me to decide if I *really* want to meet my biological family.

Now that it is time. I am no longer sure that I do.

12

Valet Service

I have waited all my life for this moment and suddenly I'm not at all sure I want my sister to know we are related. It's terrifying.

I think back once again to how I finally arrived at this day.

***

It was a snowy day in January, 1995. I was scheduled for some medical tests at Warren General Hospital. They had just instituted a parking valet service. A young woman parked my car and handed me a number. She was average height with sandy blonde hair and blue eyes. Not someone I would be likely to notice in a crowd. Her name tag read "Kim."

"When you are finished in the lab, just come out here to my window. I'll meet you and go get your car. Hope your tests go well. See ya' later." She gives me an absent-minded wave and is off to meet the next car.

When I'm finished, I return to the valet window. No one is there. Kim returns shortly and I hand her my number. She leaves to get my car but is back in less than a minute.

"Umm, we don't have this system down very good yet. Your car is blocked in by another car and I don't have the keys to it. I guess we'll just have to wait here 'til the driver returns."

We chat to pass the time. Suddenly Kim looks at me, scrutinizing my face.

"Do you know my mother?" she asks abruptly.

"I have no idea. Who is your mother?"

"Donna Bennod," she declares.

I'm so startled I don't know what to say.

Finally, I say, "No, I don't know her but I do know of her."

"Oh, well, I just thought you might know her." Kim shrugs her shoulders.

The driver of the errant car returns and drives away. Kim retrieves my car and saying, "See ya," sends me on my way.

I drive home shaken to the core.

"Jon, I just met my niece!" I call as soon as I open the back door to our house. I am dangerously close to hysteria. I feel it rising in my chest and clawing at my throat.

I explain to Jon all about Kim and how I am sure she is my niece but sometime in the feverish night I realize this probably isn't my niece at all. I am sure that if any of my children was going to ask someone if they knew me, they would refer to me as Becky Erickson—not as Becky Samuelson, not by my maiden name.

It's not my niece after all. I decide that would be too much of a coincidence.

Two days later the doctor's nurse calls. My tests are inconclusive.

Thus begins a week of return visits to the hospital. Each time I see Kim I ask her a little more about her mother.

Of course, my first question to her is, "Is Donna Bennod your mother's married name or her maiden name?"

"It's her maiden name," she answers in a voice that implies I have asked a very stupid question. "I thought you might know her from school or something. Her married name is Storie. She is married to Dick Storie. Maybe you know him? She lives in Russell, PA, but they are moving," she goes on. "In fact, she's packing right now."

Russell is only a few miles from me, my sister has only been a few miles away!

"Moving?" I look at Kim with alarm. "Where is she going?"

"Oh, they're just moving to Bemus Point. Dick's parents live there and they are getting old and need help so they are moving up there."

Bemus Point. Bemus Point is not very far away. Not as close as Russell but not far either.

I sag with relief. Yet, I say nothing. I am too afraid.

The next day I am relieved to find Kim on duty. I pose question number two. "How old is your mother?"

After briefly pondering my question, she says "Oh, I think she is 55. Yes, I know she is. She turned 55 in April."

Fifty-five: That means my sister is five years older than me and that seems to line up with what Aunt Margaret told me.

In my bed that night the day's events stomp rudely through my mind. I begin to wonder: *Does Kim know who I am? Is she fishing to see if I know about her family? What should I do? How can I find out without revealing anything if she doesn't know?* I ponder, I pray, crying out to God begging for wisdom and guidance.

In the early hours of the morning, I have a revelation as to how to approach the subject.

That day I deliberately wait until I see Kim at the valet window to take my ticket and have her retrieve my car. When she brings the car around, I am ready with my well-rehearsed speech.

"Kim, when your mother was quite young, maybe 4 or 5, my Aunt Margaret knew her. She once told me that when I was that age, I put her in mind of your mother. She said we were a lot alike. Are we still?"

Kim studies me only briefly before answering, "Nah, you are nothing like *my* mother."

That's it then. I can put my mind at ease. I am not known. I am still *in charge*. The Lord's leaving the decision as to whether I want to go on with this or not up to me. I am grateful for that grace because I really don't know if I want to open that door. Once opened, I know it can never be closed and my life would never be the same and neither would the lives of my families; married family, adopted family, birth family would all be altered forever.

It is a few days before I see Kim again. When we meet, she draws me aside, "You know, I've been thinking. You don't look at all like my mother but geez, you sure do look like my Aunt Ginny."

Then she tells me, "A couple years ago my mother learned she had a baby sister who was given away at birth. She and my Uncle David—he was the only one who believed my mom—posted notices in the Erie newspaper looking for her but they never found out anything."

"Oh, my," I say trying to sound both sympathetic and detached, "I have heard of such things before. That must have been hard for your mother."

"Yeah, it was. But, hey..."

There is nothing left for either of us to say and we part with our now traditional, "See ya."

I know I will have to make a decision to reach out to Donna through Kim or forget about my biological family because I can't go on physically or emotionally as I am. I'm not sleeping or eating well. My whole thought processes are overwhelmed with reruns of every word exchanged with Kim.

After much prayer, I write my name and phone number on a paper thinking that I will give it to Kim when I see her today and ask her to give it to her mother having her say something like, "This lady would like to meet you for coffee someday. She says you don't know her but the two of you share a number of common friends and acquaintances and it might be fun to get together and just remember some of them from the old days."

I put the paper in my jeans pocket and am on my way yet again to the hospital. My tests have been finished for a few days now. Thankfully they showed no problems. An elderly cousin of Mom's is in the hospital with a broken hip and I have become her daily visitor. She has no other family in the area and she is absolutely delighted that I have decided to take such an interest in her well-being.

I can't in good conscience use the valet service now that I am a visitor but I always see Kim. However, today there is no Kim. There is no Kim the next day and still no Kim the third day. Perhaps the Lord doesn't want me to contact my sister after all. On day four I am determined that if I don't see Kim, I will know it is not God's timing and I'll throw the paper out and never pursue the matter again.

I leave by the door where Kim and I first met and where we have talked so often. No Kim.

Slowly I walk to my car feeling a mix of sadness and relief that the Lord has given His last word on the matter. Just as I get into my car, there is a knock on the driver's side window. I put the window down. There stands Kim, her long hair blowing into her eyes, a big smile on her face.

"Hey. I haven't seen you for a few days. How are you?" she asks.

"I am doing better, thanks. Ah, Kim, I was wondering if I gave you a paper with my name and number on it, if you would ask your mother if she'd be interested in meeting for coffee someday? I know she doesn't know me but we do share a number of people and experiences. What do you think?"

I hold the now crumpled yellow lined paper in my clammy hand. Kim takes it.

"Sure, I bet she would like that. I'll have her call you. Bye. Take care."

I wait a week.

No call.

I wait two weeks.

No call.

It is well into the third week when I get a call from a woman who says she is Donna Bennod Storie.

"My daughter says I know you," she begins, "but I can't place you."

"No, you don't know me," I say feeling a little silly, "but we do know a lot of the same folks. Your brother Norrie and my husband Jon were school buddies years ago and my cousin Joyce Johnson was your neighbor. I just wondered if you might like to get together and visit."

"Well…sure," she sounds tentative. "Where would you like to meet? I'll be in Warren next Wednesday and we could meet then."

"Great! How about meeting at the Holiday Inn?" I suggest thinking to myself that we should meet in a place worthy of such a *monumental event*—as though the TV cameras and drum roll would accompany *the event*. Only I am not even sure there will be *an event* because I'm not at all sure I will tell her I'm her sister.

"No, I don't want to go to the Holiday Inn. That's too fancy for coffee. Let's meet at that hot dog place in the mall. I will meet you at 1 PM there on Wednesday. OK?"

I can hardly insist on anything else under the circumstances, so I agree.

Wednesday is five endless days away.

Now, at last, it is Wednesday.

Jon offers to come with me but I tell him, "That would seem kind of funny when we are just having a simple meeting of two people to share some old memories and have coffee. I have to go alone."

He agrees, hugs me hard and sends me on my way.

At last, the walk is over. I have reached the hot dog place. I still don't know if I will tell her or I won't tell her.

Suddenly I realize, I have no way to recognize Donna.

13

I Will Tell Her

I *have no idea what this woman looks like! I only know she doesn't look like me. How will I know her?*

I look and there in the first booth, just inside the entrance to the hot dog place and nearly in the hall of the mall itself, a woman sits alone and looking expectant.

"Donna?" I ask.

"Yes. Are you Becky?"

"I am. Thank you for meeting me."

After studying me for a moment Donna says, "I am sure that we have never met."

"No, we haven't," I agree as I slip into the booth across from her. "But your brother Norrie and my husband Jon were childhood friends and my cousin Joyce Johnson used to play with your sister Ginny when they were young. I just thought it might be fun for us to meet. I met your daughter Kim at the hospital through the new valet service."

"Yes, she told me. She said you look like my sister Ginny and she's right, you do!"

Kim is right, Donna doesn't look like me. She is small like me but bigger boned. Her hair is darker, longer and curly. She has blue eyes.

While we quietly study one another, the waitress comes over to take our order. We are the only people in the place.

"I'll just have coffee," Donna says. I order the same. When it comes, I sip the hot, strong, black liquid that burns both my throat and my stomach. Donna doctors hers with cream and sugar.

"So, tell me again how I know you," Donna says in an attempt to break the awkward silence that has fallen between us.

Once again, I tell her about my cousin Joyce, who was a neighbor of theirs.

"Oh, I remember her. She had a brother, Jim, I think his name was, didn't she?" Donna asks.

"Yes, that's them. They are my cousins."

Then I tell her about Norrie and my husband Jon being in school together, and about Jon attending a birthday party for Norrie when he was little.

Now it is time to confirm what I know concerning my family. I look at her and say, "Your brother Norrie must be 56 this year."

"No," she corrects me. "He turned 57 in May."

"That can't be!" I argue in alarm.

The thought occurs to me maybe this whole thing is just a mixed-up misunderstanding. I am terrified. I really don't have any *proof*. Then I remember Dad saying, "Your Mom said, 'That is Becky's mother.'"

I decide maybe Donna is just confused about how old her brother really is.

"Jon just turned 56 and he and Norrie were in school together so *he has to be* 56," I insist hoping this will jog her memory concerning Norrie's age.

"He is 57," she says firmly. Then she adds, "You see, when we were just little children our mother went away. I was 5, Norrie was 6. They told us she had to go out west somewhere to take care of a sick relative or something like that. We didn't know of any relatives out west but we were just little kids so we didn't question it.

"We were split up. I went to one relative and Norrie went to another. Our father was in the service, our mother was gone, and we had lost one another. Everyone in the family seemed mad about something. We figured they were mad at us but we didn't know how to make them un-mad. It was awful. As a result, Norrie failed that year in school, so from then on he was a year older

63

than most of his classmates."

Her eyes have a sad, far-away look. It is a look I recognize from my work with abused women. It is the look of someone seeing down through the years back into a time of pain and darkness. Before I can speak, she goes on, her voice echoing through the corridors of her memory.

"Our mother was gone from Thanksgiving until the next spring. I think she came home in May. When she came home, she was *different*. She clung to Norrie, petting and pampering him but didn't have anything to do with me. When I tried to climb into her lap or hug her, she would simply push me away. Emotionally and physically she just wasn't there for me. I didn't know what I had done wrong. I figured I must have been a very bad girl for my mother to go away and then come home and not love me anymore.

"One of my great comforts as a little girl was to go to my mother's bedroom and look in her dresser drawers. They contained the soft clothes she wore and the smell of her clung to them and comforted me. But in the bottom drawer I found the picture of a baby. Even at that young age, I thought it was strange that this baby's picture was stuck in a drawer. My mother had pictures of her friends' babies sitting out everywhere. Why is this baby banished to a drawer? I wondered. I took the picture and ran downstairs to her. 'Mama, look, I found this baby in your dresser! Who is she?' My mother's eyes turned dark with anger. She sounded so mean. My heart sank. 'Take the picture and put it right back where you found it and never open that drawer again!' she ordered me.

"But I did open that drawer again and again. Whenever I felt lonely, which was most of the time, I would go take out the baby and I talked to her. I told her, 'You are my baby and I will always love you. I will never leave you.'"

I sit listening to my sister's pain, watching it with my eyes, feeling it in the deepest part of my being. Our coffees grow cold, forgotten, as unwanted as my sister had been.

"Then," Donna continues, "one day, about a year before my mother died the strangest thing happened. I was walking downtown Warren, going by a jewelry store, when a man called out to me, 'Sharon!' Well of course I ignored him but he was insistent and came right up and tapped me on my shoulder.

64

When I turned around to face him, he looked and said, 'Oh, I am so sorry. You aren't who I thought you were. I thought you were someone I know who works in a jewelry store in Erie. She looks just like you.' Oh, it's ok," I told him.

"I thought it was a funny story. So, I stopped at my mother's before heading home and told her about being mistaken for some Sharon who worked in a jewelry store in Erie and she burst into tears. I was shocked.

"'Donna,' she said. 'There is something I have never told you. Years ago, I had a baby that wasn't your father's child. Her name was Sharon. She was taken away from me in Erie and I have never seen her since. When she would have been about 5, I read in the newspaper that a little girl who was 5 years old had been hit and killed by a bus in Erie. I figured that was my little girl.'

"Mom, was that the little girl whose picture was in your dresser drawer all those years?" I asked. She looked at me for a long time, then quietly said yes it was.

"Mom, I know that little girl is still alive. I can feel her. I have always loved her and I know she is not dead. I will find her for you," I told her.

"You see," Donna sighs, her voice so quiet I have to lean forward, straining to hear her, "I thought if I could just find that child for my mother, she could finally love me. But Mom died and I never found that little girl."

All my resolve to remain detached drains from me the way water drains from a broken dam—in a torrential rush. I am the key to any peace and sense of love my sister might ever know.

"Donna, I am that little girl," I say.

She just looks at me numbly.

"Donna, I am your sister. *I'm* that little girl," I say again with tears flooding down my cheeks.

She begins to sob. I sob and there in the inelegant hot dog shop in a booth practically in the hall of the mall we fall into one another's arms and cry using the cheap napkins from the chrome pop-up container to soak up our tears.

I finally notice the waitress who is looking on in alarm has slowly begun to make her way toward the telephone on the wall. I realize she is probably going to call the police or something so I get hold of myself and say to her, through sobs and hick-ups, "This is my sister. This is the first time we have ever seen one another in the whole 50 years of my life."

And now the waitress is sobbing along with us. It is a very damp affair!

14

We Had The Life

"I have to call our brother, David!" Donna insists once we have calmed down a bit. "There is a pay phone out in the hall. Come on..."

"Wait, Donna." I put a restraining hand on her. "We don't need to use the pay phone. I live right across the street from here. We can go to my house and you can call from there. Anyway, my daughter Barb works at the bank right here in the mall and we can't leave without her meeting her aunt! Oh, and I had better pay for our coffee. We don't want being arrested for theft of services to be the first public thing we do together!"

The waitress insists our coffee is on the house and she hugs both of us as we leave.

Like excited children we rush into the mall, grinning at everyone we meet, our joy blessing the world. When we get to the bank, Barb's line is open. I introduce her to her Aunt Donna.

"Sweetie," I say, totally forgetting the rules of etiquette that dictate the older person should be addressed first, "This is your Aunt Donna! Donna, meet your niece, Barb."

It is just a small branch bank. All the tellers and customers overhear my grand announcement and look at us with eyes hungry for more information.

Barb comes around the counter and gives Donna a big hug. Then one of the other customers looks at my sister, "Donna?" she asks in surprise.

"Oh, my goodness, Sally! I haven't seen you in years," Donna exclaims. "Sis, this is my old classmate and friend, Sally. Sally, this is my sister!"

Sally and I have had a long and fairly close acquaintance. She looks thunderstruck. It is obvious she is thoroughly confused and suspicious of Donna's excited proclamation that *I am her sister!*

The story has to be told once again. It is impossible for us to tell it without crying.

Then an amazing thing happens. Sally, the other bank customers, and the tellers all have tears spilling from their eyes, running down their faces. They seem as surprised by them as we are.

We finally get away from the bank and into the mall parking lot. It is such a short walk down the mall corridor and out to the parking lot that I am startled.

How did it take me so long to walk this hall only an hour ago?

Donna and I head for our respective cars only to find we have parked next to one another—both of us at the far end of the lot. She follows me home.

Jon is waiting, not knowing quite what to expect from his already emotionally overloaded wife. When we burst into the house, I introduce him to Donna—we cry again.

Jon looks from one of us to the other, noting our similarities, our differences and the joy on our faces.

"I remember you," he says to Donna, "from Junior High!"

"You probably do," my sister responds looking sheepish, "lots of people seem to. Those weren't the best years in my life."

She turns to me, anxious to move away from talk of junior high.

"Can I use your phone? Where is it? I've got to call our little brother!"

I direct Donna to the phone hanging on the dining room wall. While she calls David, I fall into Jon's arms. He holds me without saying a word. No words are necessary. We have walked this path together for a long time now.

I move to the living room motioning for her to follow once she hangs up. She nods, understanding my sign language with the familiarity of a sister.

"David isn't home from work yet but I left a message for him to call as soon as he gets home. I told his son to tell him, 'I have found our sister and her name is Rebecca!'" Donna announces when she joins me in the living room.

There is a hint of frustration in her voice. David was the only one of the siblings who believed there *was* a sister. He even helped Donna place ads in the Erie paper looking for anyone who might know Sharon. They didn't get a single response but now *the missing sister* is found and Donna needs to tell him this very minute.

I pat the sofa cushion next to me. We need to sit together, to be able to touch one another, to be reassured the other is real and really there. We sit quietly, holding hands.

Suddenly Donna turns to face me and looking deep into my eyes asks, "Were you ok? Did you have a good home? Did they take care of you? I always believed you were *my baby*—you were my comfort, my best friend and I worried about you."

"I had a wonderful home," I tell her, realizing perhaps for the first time just how wonderful my life has been and feeling just a little guilty.

"My Daddy died when I was just short of my seventh birthday. Mom brought us up alone but we had a stable, loving home. Jesus was a living, active part of our family and we depended on Him. Mom didn't have much money but she was really creative. Every holiday we celebrated with paste-on stickers of the holiday on our napkins and the appropriate color frosting on our cupcakes. I remember one year when Mom made green icing for our St Patrick's Day cupcakes. She got carried away with the food coloring and they turned out so green they glowed. All the kids sitting around me in the cafeteria laughed! It was horrifying to a junior high kid but kind of funny to remember now."

I am trying to condense my life, not wanting to take up too much of our newfound time together. It makes me sound breathless, probably because I am.

"Oh, I am so glad," she sighs. "I am glad you had a secure and happy childhood."

Once again, she seems to looks wistfully off into the past that only she can see. "I wish I had."

The phone jangles rudely in the dining room. I get up to answer it expecting it is probably David.

"Hello?" I answer brightly.

"Hello," the deep unfamiliar voice of the man at the other end of the line says. "Is this Rebecca?"

"Yes, this is she," I reply expecting him to ask for Donna.

Instead he says, "I'm your brother David. Welcome to the family!"

I can't see the man. I can only hear his voice and still tears run down my face. It seems I have a lifetime supply of them stored somewhere deep within just waiting for this day.

"I was wondering if I could come see you?" he asks.

"Certainly!" I reply. "When did you have in mind?"

"Where do you live?" he asks. "I will be there is just a few minutes."

Jon has carried on with the necessary tasks of life, preparing supper for his father who lives with us and making enough for Donna and myself as well.

"Come and eat," he calls us.

But we're so filled up with joy neither of us is hungry. However, Jon's invitation reminds Donna how late it is.

"Thanks, Jon," she says, "that is really sweet of you—I had better get home to my own husband who will be wondering what's become of me!"

Before I allow her to leave, I insist she call home and let Dick know she is on her way.

"Wait until you hear what I found today!" she exclaims excitedly into the phone. "No, I will tell you when I get there! I'll be home soon."

She hangs up on her bewildered husband.

She hugs Jon and I walk her to her car where we hug again and again. It is almost impossible to part. It has taken us fifty years to find one another and to find ourselves.

Once I am back in the house, Jon coaxes me, "Come sit down and eat something."

I finally agree but just as I pull out my chair to be seated the doorbell chimes. I jump up as though catapulted from the chair and rush to the door.

There stands a big teddy bear of a man armed with such a kind smile that it makes my heart melt.

"Rebecca?" he asks.

His eyes are blue, like Donna's. It's easy to tell they are siblings.

"David?"

Without another word he engulfs me in a hug that lifts me from my feet. It is a hug that speaks all the words that can never be spoken between us because such words don't come from the mouth, they come from the heart.

"Come in, come in," I insist.

Jon stands to greet David and introduces David to his father. Jon's dad Emil has been praying for this day to come for me for a long, long time. He smiles at my brother and gives him a firm handshake.

"Wow, you sure have a good grip for an older man!" David says in surprise, looking at my father-in-law who is 5'7", weighs only 130 pounds and is 86 years old. Emil grins in delight.

"We were just going to eat," Jon says. "Won't you join us?"

I am relieved when David declines saying he has just eaten. I don't want to share this moment with Emil or even Jon. I want this moment, this brother, all to myself.

"Let's go into the living room." I wave my hand vaguely in that direction but David is worried that I will be missing my supper.

"I am not a single bit hungry," I tell him honestly. "Come on."

I grab his hand and pull him with me toward the living room like a small child impatiently pulling on her brother.

We sit on the sofa in the same order Donna and I sat. I am to his right. He turns toward me and looks me over.

"Sis, did you have a good life?" he asks. "Were you treated well? Were you OK?"

I reassure him, as I had Donna, that my life has been good. He sighs.

"I am so glad," he finally says.

We talk and talk. David tells me about the difficult years of his life that had him living back with his parents a few years ago. I also learn that David collects teddy bears, Matchbox cars, and hugs, all with equal passion. It is easy to see that although he is a fine, responsible, grown man, he has managed to retain a childlike joy and an innocent, fierce love.

Perhaps for the first time in my life I truly begin to see that, despite all the grief I have experienced, I had a wonderful childhood, safe and faith-filled. I am painfully becoming aware that my siblings were not equally blessed.

David produces a handful of snapshots from a pocket.

"This is your family," he says as he hands them to me.

One by one he tells me who is who and when the different pictures had been taken: There is Norrie and his wife, Beverly as young people; our mother with our sister Virginia; Donna as a child playing with a rabbit; David himself as a little tyke; our mother and her husband celebrating an anniversary.

"Oh, David, this is wonderful," I exclaim. Then I tentatively ask, "Could I keep them just long enough to have copies made?"

"Nope!" he answers looking very solemn. Then he breaks into the infectious grin I will come to love. "I brought them for you to keep. We had the life and the memories. You only have the pictures. They are yours," he tells me while folding his big hand around my small one holding the precious pictures of a past that I will only know from stories.

Soon after that he informs me that he has to leave. I hug him again and again while more tears flow from my endless supply. It has been an over-whelming day.

Once David's car has pulled out of the driveway, I discover I am starved. I sit down at the table and Jon brings my warmed-over supper to me.

The next day there is a call from Norrie.

"Hi, Sis. Donna said she had found our sister. Wow! Well, welcome. We live in Florida but we'll be coming up there for Christmas. Can't wait to meet you in person. I remember Jon. That's really neat. Anyway, we'll be seeing you soon! Bye for now!"

(I suppose I must have said something. I am seldom without words but while I can still hear my brother's voice in my memory, I have no recollection of anything I said. I guess I was still pretty much in shock.)

Now there is only Ginny—Ginny, the sister who looks like me. Ginny, the sister I am pretty sure is my missing half. I am so anxious to meet Ginny or at least talk with her. But that will have to wait.

15

Sharing My Story

Several times a day I look through the pictures David has given me. I am struck by how much my younger sister Virginia, Ginny, looks like me when we were young.

I long to hear from her, to meet her but there is no phone call, no word of any kind.

When I ask Donna, she says in a vague manner, "I just don't know what is wrong with her, honey. She won't talk about it and doesn't want to hear anything about you. I'm sorry. Sometimes she is just that way."

Donna, David and Kim all insist over and over again, "You look just like Ginny!"

Now I find myself wondering if my little sister feels displaced by all the excitement about *finding a sister who looks just like her* and lives right here among them while she's living in Kentucky and seldom sees any of the family.

The more I think about it, the more I am sure that if it was me in her shoes, I would feel resentful and left out and angry. I debate about sending her a note but Donna and David both tell me it would be best just to let her come around in her own time.

I struggle with my sympathy for Ginny and the fact that at long last, my *twin* is within reach and she wants nothing to do with me. The pain is actually physical, making my whole body ache, as though I have the flu.

Donna calls a week later and invites me to their house for lunch.

"Give me very specific directions, I am directionally challenged," I tell her. "I can get lost inside a paper bag."

"It's genetic, Sis," she says laughing at me. But she does give me very careful directions right down to the big identifying rock in front of the house.

It feels like I am driving forever and just about the time I am sure I am hopelessly lost I see the rock!

As I drive into the driveway and stop the car, I am greeted by two huge dogs, growling and barking. I'm tempted to back out of the driveway and head back home as quickly as I can. I'm terrified by *little barking dogs*. These great beasts threaten an end to my relationship with my sister before it has begun.

Donna yells at them, "Girls, stop it. That's *a kid*! Come on in, Sis. Don't pay any attention to them. They are just big babies. They won't hurt you."

Every human I have ever known who has dogs says that about their animal and I know it's a lie! My own Chihuahua-mix once lit into a police officer who came to the door to see Jon about some piano parts. Fortunately, the officer was wearing high leather boots and his ankle remained unscathed.

These dogs were big enough to rip out my throat without even stretching. I stubbornly refuse to open my door. Donna calls the dogs again. This time they listen and slink behind her. Love wins over fear, I exit the car.

Once we are inside, the dogs settle. It seems since my sister has let me in the house and repeatedly reassured them that I am *a kid*, they must consider me to be part of the family and therefore need not be dispensed with today.

I sit in a kitchen chair. It's padded and has wheels. I pull the chair as close to the table as I can get it—that makes me *feel* safer. The dogs sniff me once and lope off to another room. I pray they stay there.

Donna has coffee cups, sugar, cream and napkins beside the coffee pot on the counter.

"Coffee, Sis?" she asks. "Do you use cream or sugar? I can't remember anything about how you took your coffee at the mall!"

"Black, thank you," I say.

I would really like to get out of the chair and help her but I am afraid if I move the dogs will be back. I remain glued to the chair while my sister brings cups of steaming coffee and pretty napkins to the table.

Despite the dogs, I feel completely at home. It's as though we've been doing this for years. Over the strong, hot coffee we compare our lives. We learn we are both hairdressers who went to beauty school in our thirties. We both love to sew and make some of our own clothes and clothes for our girls.

"I love to can," Donna tells me. "Dick and I have a big garden and from mid-summer until late fall I can stuff—or put it in the freezer. Dick hunts, so we often have venison for the freezer. And we buy meat raised locally—a half-side of beef or pork and put that in the freezer."

"So do we!" I exclaim. "Well, truth be told, I used to can more than I do now but we have venison in the freezer and buy a half-side of pork and one of beef. Amazing!"

We learn we even use the same butcher, Caffaro's in Sugar Grove. It seems the harder we try to find differences, the more we find we are alike.

However, as we begin to talk about our childhood experiences and our marriages, the differences soon become evident.

At her insistence, I tell my story first. After all, she is the older sister and used to being boss. I chafe at that a bit. In my family, I am the older sister and used to being the boss, but our relationship is new and I am unwilling to test its strength, so I begin to tell my story.

She cries when I tell her about those first seven years of my life.

"But what about the rest of your life? Was it all that sad and hard?" she asks anxiously.

"No," I say. "Actually, it was pretty good over-all although we did have one or two more serious scares before we got to be grown-ups."

I confess, "Sometimes I resented having to be the *babysitter* for all my growing up years and I thought my mother expected a lot from me but I realize that it wasn't so bad."

Donna nods knowingly.

"Becky, tell me about it," she insists. "How can I *know* my sister if I don't know anything about all those lost years?"

So, I begin.

"When Debbie was in kindergarten, in February of 1956, Mom was stricken with Asian flu. Once again, relatives and neighbors came and took care of us; making sure we had meals and clean clothes, and were never alone. Mom lay in bed, pale and weak. I was nearly eleven and ramped up my attempts to take care of everybody. And I worried what would become of my brother and sister if Mom died.

"My Aunt Margaret reassured me that 'if anything happens to your mother, you know you will always have a home with us.'

"What I *heard* was. 'If anything happens to your mother, you know that *you* will always have a home with us.'

"In my young mind, perhaps because I knew about their earlier attempt to dissuade my mother from keeping my brother, I was sure the two little ones would be sent away. I worried and fretted and tried to figure out how I could keep us all together if Mom died. Every day I was grateful I was a day older and closer to 18, an age I imagined would allow me to keep them myself. It was a long and scary seven years until I actually got there."

Donna is listening intently, murmuring in agreement, "I know just how you felt. Go on."

I continue, "Mom slowly began to regain strength. She'd get out of bed for short periods of time but wasn't feeling strong enough to get dressed or to take care of us. One day my sister came home from kindergarten and went into Mom's bedroom. Instead of going to the bed to see Mom, she went to the closet where she pulled at one of Mom's house dresses hanging there and said, 'I wish some day when I came home you would be wearing this.' Mom told me about it one day when we were remembering that time.

"Mom said that was the turning point for her. The next day she got out of bed and put on the house dress and when Debbie came home from school, she was at the door to meet her. Once Debbie was in first grade, Mom went to work part-time for the Warren Observer. Do you remember when it was a weekly newspaper?" I ask Donna.

"Sure, I do, Sis."

"Well, Mom was a proof-reader and was exceptional at spotting errors in spelling, grammar, or misplaced ads. It did her a world of good to be part of the grown-up world again, not only earning money but contributing to society. She loved that job. Before too long, her skills were noticed by others and she was offered the job of secretary for the elementary school that my brother and sister were attending. I was at Beaty Junior High by then. We were finally making it. And we had some fun times.

"We took trips to see my Aunt Mary and Uncle Carl in Rochester. Their home once again became a happy place in my mind. It took us two days to get there," I say laughing, "because Mom got tired from driving and I was still vomiting on a regular basis whenever we drove more than 20 miles at a time, but once we were there we all had such fun. Aunt Mary still enveloped me in a fragrant hug and called me *Honey Child*," I recall.

"We kids played in the yard and the adults had cocktails on the patio before dinner—shocking to me because at home neither Mom nor Auntie drank but Mom would sparkle with the joy of being looked after, so I didn't care. Eventually, I would learn that Uncle Carl sent a generous check to Mom every year at Christmas to be used to buy gifts not only for us kids but for her to get something for herself, as well. I don't think any of his siblings ever knew he did that. None of them had any extra to do so and maybe he even sent checks to them too. I don't know."

I fear I am rambling and boring my new sister with such meandering into my past but she encourages me to continue.

"Auntie, that's what we called my Aunt Evelyn, my father's sister—she was a maiden lady—always came along on our trips. While she didn't like to drive, she did know how and had a driver's license, giving comfort to Mom that there was at least another *potential* driver in the car, and Auntie always paid for the gas and our motel room. We carried food with us and picnicked as we went. In those days there were many public picnic areas, most with covered pavilions, so we could picnic even if it was raining.

"On a more regular basis, we'd go visit Aunt Margaret and Uncle Jim. They had moved back from Cleveland and lived in Endeavor, in the home where she'd grown up. Her mother was old and had cancer of the eye. They came home to care for her. The trip there was only 30 miles, but Mom always packed a picnic and we'd stop at a picnic area to eat about half-way there so I wouldn't get sick."

At the mention of Aunt Margaret, Donna stops me.

"Is that the same person who told you about me?" she asks. "She must be very special. I hope I can meet her soon. We really do have to get together."

"Yes, we do—we really do. She would love to meet you," I tell her.

"Anyway, we loved going to Aunt Margaret and Uncle Jim's house. The people next door had a barn and horses. Debbie was absolutely crazy about horses and my brother Jimmy loved them as well. We would go and play in the barn with the blessing of the farmer who lived there. Uncle Jim loved to cook and would make big fluffy buckwheat pancakes or there would be a savory pot roast awaiting our arrival, and despite our picnic-on-the-way we all ate like we hadn't seen food for a week!"

I am sitting at my sister's table but my mind has gone far back into the past. Donna is leaning forward absorbing every word. It's almost as though she is living those happy days with me, so I keep on talking.

"They were both the best and worst of times all tangled together in my mind. Fear and joy were so mixed sometimes it was hard to sort one emotion from the other. But overriding it all was my mother's unshakable faith in God and her trust that no matter what, He would take care of us.

"Jesus wasn't a *concept* in our house, He was a real presence. When we had a crisis or a need or a wonderful joy, we told Him about it. Whenever we were bad, we confessed aloud to Him right then and there. We went to church every Sunday. Mom taught Sunday school and the all the little kids in her class just loved her.

"One parent told her that as they were driving by the church one day, their child said, 'Oh, look, there's where God and Dorothy live!' It was a story she loved to tell."

"Wouldn't it be wonderful if we could all get together for a meal sometime? I would love to meet your Aunt Margaret," Donna interjects.

I am embarrassed. I have been talking for way too long.

"Speaking of meals," Donna says. "I am starved, Sis, and you must be too. I have lunch in the refrigerator. You can set the table. The silverware is in that drawer right over there. There are bigger napkins are on the counter. I'll just put our food on our plates. Do you want more coffee or is water OK?"

I assure her if I have any more coffee I will be jumping out of my skin. She gets the food ready. Tentatively I stand up. The dogs pay no attention. I set the table. We move in tandem as though we had done this forever.

After lunch, I *will insist* that she tell me her story—older sister or not!

16

A Thousand Hugs

It feels so natural to be working side by side with my sister in her kitchen that it makes my heart ache. *How much we have missed*, I think sadly but then I realize I don't know anything about my sister's life. I have no idea what we have missed.

When the dishes are done, we refill our glasses with ice and water and return to the kitchen table. It is here we feel safe and connected.

"Donna, it's your turn," I say.

"My turn?" She puts an innocent look on her face as though she has no idea what I mean.

"I just made lunch, that was my turn," she says sweetly.

"Well, Smarty, I helped with the dishes. In fact, I put the last dish in the dishwasher, so now it's your turn again. And you know what I mean. I want to hear your story."

Donna sighs and begins, "Well, I remember playing at the playground in the summer, when I was little. And sled riding in the winter. Those are my happiest memories."

She looks at me brightly to see if this will be enough to satisfy me. It isn't.

"Yes," I say, "And?"

Somewhat reluctantly she continues, "Well, I already told you that Mom went away when I was four. I was sent to Great Aunt Emma's house and Norrie was sent to our Bennod grandparents. That was an awful time and I really don't want to talk about it again."

"That's OK, Donna," I reassure her. "I understand perfectly, but tell me about your life after that."

"Well, my little sister Ginny was born when I was seven—I always called her *the brat*, I still do."

My heart gives a little lurch—I hope my sister doesn't notice the look that has just swept over my face because I don't want her to think I am judging, but in *my family* we would never have been allowed to call one another *brat* and Mom never once called any of us that. I feel sorry for my younger sister having to grow up being called *the brat* but then I realize that Donna herself had probably been called *brat*. I feel so sad.

"Four years after Ginny was born, David was born. Even though Norrie is two years older than I am, I was *the girl* so I was expected to help Mom with the babies and with the housework. Mom never treated me as though she loved me or even cared for me after what I realize now was the time the baby was taken from her in Erie. She never hugged me or told me she loved me. That was all I ever wanted—just to be noticed and loved but it didn't happen."

Donna's voice is laden with sorrow. I reach out and take her hand.

Her eyes mist over as she continues. "Dad was a very sick person—actually, he was a child molester. I didn't know—I just didn't know it was wrong—what he was doing to me. I could never figure out why my friends' parents wouldn't let them come to my house—or even play with me, but it seems everyone *knew* about Dad and they didn't let their kids come to our house and they didn't want me around their kids. But no one tried to help me. No one reported him. I guess that's how it was back then. The father *owned* the kids and could do whatever he wanted with them.

"By the time I was eleven years old, I was dating older boys. I never let them, well you know—get intimate or anything because I thought they would somehow…know. Then they would think bad of me."

My heart bangs wildly in my chest; a ball of something horrible rises in my throat and threatens to choke me. My first thought is: How did my sister ever endure her childhood? Then I wonder: If this had happened to my sister, her father's biological child, what in dear God's name would he have done with me? My lungs burn with a desperate need for oxygen but I can't seem to remember how to breathe. It seems as though I hear my sister's voice far off in the distance, continuing with her story. I will myself to breathe, to listen as she continues.

"I met my first husband, Ron, when I was 14. We met roller skating. He was 21. We dated for a year then I got pregnant. Dad insisted we get married. I didn't want to marry Ron because I knew he was running around with other girls but when I told Dad I wasn't going to get married he told me, 'You don't have a choice. I already signed over your guardianship to Ron.'

"We were married December 31—New Year's Eve, 1955. In April I turned sixteen and in May gave birth to our first child, a baby girl. Ron liked to drink and he continued to run around with other girls. I knew it but there was nothing I could do about it."

She suddenly looks at me with an astonished expression, as though it's the first time she has thought of this.

"Do you realize that today Ron would have been convicted of statutory rape? He could have been sent away to prison! Of course, Dad would never have pressed charges. He was glad to be rid of me.

"The first two years were really hard. We bought land with a cabin on it—an old hunting camp, probably. It just had two rooms: no sink or stove except a three-burner oil burning thing. We had to bring water in buckets from a spring that was quite a distance from the cabin. And we had an outhouse. And that's where we lived in the summer."

Now that she has begun her story, my precious sister charges on determined to get it all said before it creeps back into the darkness where it has lived and eaten away at her for years.

"In the winter we lived in a little camping trailer with no water or heat. Ron bought a wood stove and built a small shed at the back door of the trailer. That would probably have been alright but the wood he cut to burn was green and it sat smoldering, filling the place with more smoke than heat.

"That poor baby spent most of her first winter in bed. I piled blankets on her to try and keep her warm. Sometimes I would put her in our bed and cuddle around her—trying to warm and comfort both her and me. I wanted her to know that even if she was cold, I loved her.

"Oh, that's enough of that. There is so much more—melting snow for water to wash diapers and our clothes. But, eventually, things did get better as I got older. We had two more children and I had four miscarriages. Through it all, I never forgot the picture of the baby in my mother's dresser. She was my comfort. And now, here you are!"

I get up from the table, never giving the dogs a single thought and walk behind my sister's chair. I put my arms around her and lay my head on hers. I just want to hold her forever, to give her a thousand hugs, to somehow make it all better.

With all my heart I wish I could absorb some of her pain, some of the poison that's been thrown on her over the years of her life. It seems so unfair. I had such a good life—although I hadn't known just how good it was until now—while she had suffered. None of what had happened to her was her fault. She has no reason to feel guilt or shame yet I can tell both guilt and shame are hanging onto her like a vicious dog that can't be shaken.

Still, in spite of all she had been through, my sister is strong. She is a beautiful woman inside and out. And she has found the courage to show me her woundedness. She trusts me. I hug her tight and cry.

"Donna," I finally say, "I don't know how you survived all that. You are amazing."

"I didn't do it alone," she assures me. "I always had Jesus. I always knew He was right there with me. When I was little my Grandma Erickson—I don't think she was related to Jon's Erickson family—took me to church. I went to Sunday school and to Bible school for a little while and I knew about Jesus. He was my friend. I have always talked to Him and He has always been right beside me. I don't know why but I never blamed Him for any of what happened to me. Even as a child I knew it wasn't His fault and that He didn't like it happening so He stayed really close and gave me absolute faith and trust in Him. Without Him I wouldn't be here today."

My sister and I had so many differences growing up yet here is our common denominator, Jesus.

I happen to glance at the clock on the stove and I'm shocked to see it's nearly five! Where have the hours gone? It's dark outside and I hate to drive in the dark. I need to get home. Jon will be worried.

"Oh gosh, Sis! Look at the time! I have to go home but may I use your phone to call Jon before I leave? He's going to wonder what's become of me!"

"Certainly, you may use the phone, Sister. What a silly question," she says with a laugh.

"Well, it is long distance. I can pay for the call," I offer.

She bops me on the head with the newspaper that's lying on the counter. "You are impossible! And I love you. I can't thank God enough, ever, for bringing us together."

"Amen!" I say.

After calling Jon and about a thousand more hugs, I leave for home but not before making plans to come again in two weeks. I have a car, Donna doesn't. It is easier for me to come to her.

"Next time," Donna says as she is closing my car door, "we need to make plans for all of us to get together."

I nod in agreement, far too tired and overwhelmed to think of plans-in-the-future but we do promise to meet again in two weeks.

17

My Turn Again

When I arrive at Donna's two weeks later the dogs merely look at me. Still not trusting them completely, I once again roll myself close to the kitchen table, but this time I have helped myself to coffee and poured a cup for my sister first.

"It's your turn..." Donna says as she gives me that *big sister look*.

"What? I just poured the coffee so it's your turn," I say in my most smarty-sister voice, knowing full well what she means.

"Rebecca!"

"OK, what do you want to know?"

"Did you go to school after high school? How old were you when you got married? How did you meet Jon?"

One of the dogs comes to sniff me. I tentatively pat her on the head. She sighs and lies down at my feet. I bury my nose in the steam rising from my cup, enjoying its rich aroma. The steam rising from the hot coffee triggers so many memories.

"I can't ever remember not knowing Jon. Our parents were friends long before I was adopted, so I guess when I was adopted, Jon met me," I say with a little laugh. "I have no memory of life without knowing him. We went to the same church and I even have a picture of our two families on some outing when I was just a little girl. We began to date when I was 17 and he was just about to turn 23.

"I graduated from high school and went to nursing school in Washington, DC. It was a government program and it was tuition free. The only catch was, if there was a war, we would be called up to serve—even if we hadn't graduated yet."

"I didn't know you are a nurse!" Donna exclaims in surprise.

"I'm not. I never was. Oh, I loved the schooling and did really well academically for the first year, but once we began to work on the floors I knew nursing wasn't for me. What I really wanted to do was to sit and hear the patients' life stories. I longed to find a way to bring them hope.

"Capital City School of Nursing was associated with DC General Hospital, a hospital for the indigent. This was 1963 before the Civil Rights act was passed in 1964. Many Blacks were forced to live in horrible conditions while paying really high rents. Most didn't have good jobs and couldn't afford medical care. They didn't go for medical care until it was a crisis. That's when we saw them. I was shocked to see people in those conditions—especially in our nation's capital!

"I came from "White" Warren—what did I know about the situation of Black people or about racial injustice? All I knew was that what I was seeing and hearing for the first time in my life was so wrong. And I just wanted to give those poor patients a chance to tell their stories, to really be seen and heard. I wanted to pray for them and sometimes I did right then and there.

"I don't have to tell you that didn't go down well with the nursing instructors! I got bawled out for spending too long with patients, for talking when I was supposed to be working, and I knew beyond any shadow of a doubt, I was not cut out to be a nurse."

"I know what you mean," Donna says. "I went to nursing school in Erie for a year and I was only too happy to quit. It wasn't for me either."

"Really?" Now it's my turn to be astonished.

Another thing we share. This is really kind of weird. Three kids each: two daughters and a son, nursing school drop-outs, beauty school successes, oldest daughters who took charge of our siblings, a love of sewing and even canning...

"Go on, Sis," my sister says. "I didn't mean to interrupt. Did you get married then?"

I chuckle and go on with my story. "My mother would never approve of my leaving school to get married—never! She was determined that I would have a career in case I ended up having to support my children in the future. I didn't care. All I knew was that I wasn't staying in nursing school. Jon and I talked on the phone every few days and when I told him I was going to leave school, he tried to talk me into staying. He couldn't. He had asked me to marry him at Christmas when he gave me my engagement ring. So, I figured it was okay to say that if he really wanted to marry me, this would be a good time to do it because I was leaving school no matter what!

He was quick to remind me that my mother would never agree! We would have to elope. There wouldn't be a big church wedding. He was worried I might regret that someday. I really didn't care. I was so happy. 'That is fine with me,' I told him."

I paused to take a breath and check to see where the dogs had gotten to. Reassured that they were still ignoring me, I continued with the wedding story. "Because Memorial Day was only two weeks away, we decided that Jon would come to DC. No one would find it strange that he would use his long weekend to visit me. Memorial Day was on Saturday that year so he had Friday off to compensate for the holiday being on a weekend. The bonus was we would always be able to remember our anniversary because it was on a national holiday. Then they went and changed the holiday to the last Monday of May, wouldn't you know? I had no idea how to go about making arrangements. But one of my fellow nursing students, Susie, had a sister who had just eloped. I didn't dare tell Joyce because I knew she would feel duty-bound to tell my mother. That was the hardest thing, to keep it from Joyce. We had always shared everything."

"Joyce?" my sister asked in surprise. "Was she there with you, in nursing school?"

We had been sitting at the table a long time. I stood up to stretch my legs. The dogs, thankfully, paid no attention. "Yes," I said, "Joyce applied and was accepted at the school. It made it easier for both of us, being together so far from home. You can imagine how careful I had to be that she didn't catch wind of my plan. So, with Susie promising absolute secrecy, she and I went off to the courthouse together to apply for the marriage license. The legal age for marriage was eighteen. I was terrified that I would have to show my birth certificate to prove my age. I didn't have it, of course. But when the clerk of courts asked how old I was, and I told her I was nineteen, she never asked for proof. I guess they thought if you said you were eighteen, you were lying, but if you said you were nineteen you were probably telling the truth. Who knows? Anyway, I got the license and Jon and I were married in the Georgetown Methodist Church by The Reverend Doctor Haskell Deal, pastor emeritus. He was an old Swede who had just returned from a trip to Sweden. He looked at our marriage license and declared that Samuelson and Erickson sounded like a couple of good Swedes to him. 'You will do just fine,' he told us and that was the total sum of our marriage counseling."

"Smart man," Donna said, laughing. "I guess he knew what he was talking about. You two have been married a long time now, haven't you? What, thirty-one years?"

I nod absentmindedly, my mind still lost in the past. At Donna's prompting I continue. "Susie's sister's name was Donna and her new husband's name was Ron. They had agreed to be our witnesses. Wow, that is strange! I just realized that is your name and your first husband's name. Weird. The neat part of it was that we were married just an hour or so before a big wedding was to take place. The organist was practicing for that wedding and said she might as well practice the wedding march. So, Donna and I marched down the aisle to Felix Mendelssohn's "**Wedding March**" in C major. I was dressed in my white confirmation dress and a little white hat with a veil. The church was beautifully decorated with ribbons and flowers. The only thing we didn't get to do was light the candles. I've always said that whoever the bride was that got married that day paid for a *used wedding!*"

My sister laughs aloud. *She gets it. She has the same sense of humor I have.* I am delighted.

"Oh, Sister," she says, "I love it! But what about your mother? I'll just bet she wasn't very happy." (From the moment we met, Donna and I have called each other sister. I think it has to do with the preciousness of finding one another after all the years of not having one another. In fact, all we siblings call each other, brother or sister or sis. It ties us together firmly and forever.)

I shake my head, remembering my mother's fury. "Oh, my word, she was *not happy!* She threatened to have the marriage annulled when Jon went to see her. I told him to wait and we would tell her together. I was going to be home the next weekend for a friend's wedding. But Jon knew Mom would have a fit and so he chose to go and take the brunt of her anger alone. He never told me exactly what she said—he said he loved me too much to tell me. He never has. She marched off to see our pastor in Warren who pointed out to her she had two choices: to lose a daughter or to gain a son. That week she put our wedding announcement in the paper. On the weekend, I came home and she had a small reception for us on Sunday afternoon, then I went back to school. Jon stayed on in Warren. He had a job at the post office. He told me he could probably get a transfer to DC if I would stay in school. I tried. I really did try. In August, when the school closed to give students and staff a month of vacation, I came home. Jon and I took our delayed honeymoon. After that, I knew for sure I didn't want to go back to school which was wise because Kris was born nine months later," I confess with a little laugh.

"Jon still asks me if I have ever been sorry that I quit nursing. I always assure him that I have absolutely never once regretted quitting or marrying him."

Donna nods in understanding and takes our now empty coffee cups to refill them. She brings them back along with a plate of blueberry muffins she has just taken from the oven. I realize I am hungry. We both butter our muffins liberally. Another thing we share—the love of real butter, lots of it! For a while we sit quietly, treasuring one another's company, sipping coffee and ummmming over muffins but finally, at Donna's insistence I go on with my life story.

"Of course, our marriage has had its share of ups and downs—some of the downs were more like axle shattering potholes, but we've made it through. You see, I married a motor-cycle guy who wore crazy hats and red suspenders and made me laugh, but I got so much more. One day Jon said he missed playing the piano. 'You miss playing the piano?' I asked him, totally shocked. I didn't know he played the piano. We had a church key, so I suggested we go to the church and he could play there. We went. I expected him to play chop-sticks or something. Instead he played some amazing Chopin piece from memory. I sat on the steps leading to the choir loft enthralled, thinking to myself, *I bought the field and got the treasure buried in it, as well.* Even though Jon and I grew up in that church together and he had played for Sunday school before going into the Navy, I never knew he played. He's six years older than me. I suppose I was in the back room with the little kids when he was playing for the adults who had Sunday school in the sanctuary. After he went into the Navy, he quit playing until that surprising day.

"I am telling you, Sis, it was crazy. I wish you could have seen the look on our pastor, Frank Hagberg's face when he came into the sanctuary to see who was playing. He was as astonished as I was. After that Jon was playing in church every Sunday and still is. I was a Sunday school teacher and still am. Jon's mom had been the church organist—my Mom a Sunday school teacher. We still go to the same church we grew up in. We've carried on our family legacies, I guess. When the kids were in junior high, I think it was, I became a hair dresser and here we are," I conclude, tired of hearing my own voice and not wanting to bore my sister with any more details.

We have finished our coffee and eaten at least two muffins apiece—maybe more. Thankfully they weren't in papers so there isn't any concrete evidence of who has eaten how many. I suspect I have eaten the majority.

"Wouldn't it be wonderful if we could all get together for Thanksgiving?" Donna asks once I am quiet. "I just don't know where we could meet because there will be so many of us. I want you to meet my son and my two daughters and their kids and David's family and I hope your family will come too because I want to meet them...especially your Aunt Margaret!" she says all in one big breath.

"It's a wonderful idea," I agree.

But we soon discover that no one in either of our families has a place big enough for all of us.

"I can ask our church board if my—err, *our* family can use the fellowship hall for our dinner on Thanksgiving Day," I say after some thought.

"Awesome! Do you think they'll let us?" Donna asks.

"I'll call as soon as I get home," I promise. "And speaking of getting home, I really need to go. You know when I'm here time just goes so fast. We have a life-time to make up for and even we can't talk fast enough to fit a life time into these visits!"

The dogs have gone off to the bedroom and fallen asleep. I say, "Let sleeping dogs lie."

Donna shakes her head at her scaredy-cat sister and reluctantly goes to get my coat from the bedroom.

She walks me to the car and I promise to let her know as soon as I have an answer on our using the church. It feels good to have a plan. I turn on the radio and sing along with the music all the way home.

18

Thanksgiving And Beyond

As soon as I get home, I call the chairman of the church. I explain how I have met my biological family and I ask if our family can use the fellowship hall for dinner on Thanksgiving Day. My excitement over the whole event is catchy. Jerry, the church chairman tells me he will call the members of the board and get back to me as soon as possible.

The next day he calls. "Well, Becky, the board that can seldom agree on anything has agreed without a single vote of dissent to let you use Fellowship Hall and the kitchen—without charge—and they even offered to set up the tables and chairs."

"Thank you, thank you, thank you," I enthuse.

Then I call Donna to share the good news.

"We have less than two weeks to convince our families to cooperate. I hope some of them will come," I say to her.

"Oh, Sis, they'll all come! I have been telling them all about you. They can't wait to meet you. Don't worry! Oh, and I think we should all cook our turkeys and make our gravy and bring them with us. Then we will combine all the meat and mix all the gravy together and there will be no way for anyone to judge anyone else's cooking," Donna says.

I wonder if she thinks her cooking won't come up to some imaginary standard…or that mine won't.

"What a good idea!" I agree.

The day before Thanksgiving, Jon and I cook our turkey. He carves it from the bones and stores it in the refrigerator. I make the gravy, chattering nervously about the next day.

I needn't have worried no one would come. The Fellowship Hall quickly fills with the smell of fragrant food and wet wool as people pour in the door stomping snow from their boots and spilling down the stairway to the basement rooms. There are amazed exclamations as relatives, who have known each other for years but didn't know they were related, meet.

Overwhelmed, I try to hide in the kitchen busying myself with familiar tasks, but Donna grabs me and I'm propelled from person to person.

"This is your Aunt Becky! This is David's son, Scott, oh and my daughter Kim and her husband Mike and…"

I am so confused I hardly know *who I am*!

"Where is Aunt Margaret? Is she here? She is coming, isn't she?" Donna demands to know.

"She's here. Come on, I'll introduce you. But Donna, you have to calm down. I am getting all mixed up!" I exclaim. "We need nametags and relationship tags!"

Eventually, after many more confusing introductions, all accompanied by hugs, Donna and I get back to the kitchen. We cook the potatoes in a huge pot we find in the cupboard and then discover there is no potato masher. Our husbands and sons come into the already crowded kitchen to *help*. They take turns squashing and mixing the potatoes with spoons and knives and meat forks amid peals of laughter.

The turkey is piled high on platters. The gravy is mixed all together and heated in a kettle. We taste it and agree, there has never been any gravy that is better than our collective gravy.

More of our various brood arrive, side dishes in hand. Once again, I am herded by my big sister, introduced, hugged, and welcomed.

I cry, the endless tears of joy that come from an unfathomable source deep within.

From the kitchen, I look out on our combined families.

My adopted sister Debbie's son already knows my half-brother David's son. In fact, they have been friends for many years. Now they are trying to decide if they are cousins, but with all the intricate steps of half-siblings and adopted siblings, they give up and slap each other on the shoulder yelling, "Hi Cuz!" every time they cross paths.

While it is true that Donna doesn't look a thing like me, she and my sister Debbie could easily pass for sisters.

My brother Jim has declined to come. I am sorry. I would love to have him and his family here but I can respect his feelings. I know he has never understood my need to find this family. Mom was always enough for him and I think he feels I have somehow betrayed Mom.

Mom has been gone for three years now. My birth mother died five years ago. I am both a little sorry that neither can be here and yet, also relieved. I know God's timing was perfect. When my birth siblings say, "I wish you could have known our mother," I remind them that the Lord had a reason for his timing and one day we will all meet together on the other side where it won't cause either mother pain.

Aunt Margaret and my step-father, Dave, are here. They're both in their 80s and struggle to walk but everyone seeks them out at the table where they are seated—honorary matriarch and patriarch of this new family.

It is absolutely weird. There are thirty-five of us. Everyone from my biological side of the family seems to know someone from my adopted side of the family! To the best of my knowledge I am the only person in the room who has never met any of my biological family. It's as though God has kept me in a bubble all the preceding fifty years of my life—just for this moment!

The room rings with happy chatter, boisterous laughter, memories brought forth and memories being made. Love is as tangible as the smell of turkey, filling up the space and at times, literally taking away my breath. And while I have yet to meet Norrie and his wife Bev, they have promised to visit us during the Christmas Holiday season.

True to their promise, Norrie and Bev come to Warren just before Christmas.

Norrie is shorter and more-slight-in-build than David. He has an energetic manner of moving and speaking, not soft like David. You can tell he is the oldest child, although he backs down to Donna, who is unquestionably the boss of the family.

When Norrie sees Jon, he pumps his hand recalling memories from their shared lives long ago. Where David enfolds, Norrie charges: They both make sure I know I am loved and wanted.

Bev is half Native American with a quiet manner, dark smiling eyes and long black hair she pulls back and wraps into a knot at the back of her head. She shyly welcomes me to the family.

I am not sure what to do about Christmas presents for my new family but I know I want to do something. So, I write a poem which I print and frame for each of my siblings. I give them wrapped in paper and love to Donna, to David, and to Norrie. I mail one to Ginny along with a card.

Looking For You

I searched for you in the eyes of everyone I passed,
Handing out smiles like calling cards—in case it was you.
I wanted you to know I would love you, accept you
And I wanted you to love me.
In the process of meeting every eye
Smiling into all those faces—
Some gentle, some hurt, some sullen and angry—
I found hundreds of brothers and sisters.
And I was blessed by seeing light come into dull eyes,
Faces glowing with smiles
Returning the love I was freely giving,
While looking for you.
Love, Becky Erickson 1995

I wait, hoping against hope for some word from Ginny. None comes.

Finally, one day, I trudge through the snow to the mailbox. I open it expecting the usual assortment of junk mail and bills. They are there but mixed in with them is a polite little thank you note from Ginny. My sister's good manners have overcome her absolute refusal to acknowledge my existence.

I nearly wear the little note out reading and rereading it, fingering my sister's handwriting, breathing in the scent of it—even though any scent of her that might have been there is long gone.

In the spring, I decide we will *go to* the sister—the one who they say looks just like me. I can wait no longer to meet her.

Jon and I plan a camping trip for May. We will go to Kentucky. Our trip will include a visit to the Kentucky Horse Farm in Lexington, Kentucky where my sister Virginia lives.

I plan, pack and repack and I pray—Oh, how I pray that once I am there, she will agree to meet me.

19

Pink Bath Towels

May, 1996. It is finally time for our trip. I have maps and a "TripTik" from AAA, a long map with everything we will need to know about the roads between Warren and Lexington. I am armed with travel books, campground books, cook books, reading books, and enough snacks to feed a horde of travelers despite that fact that it is just Jon and me. We never go on vacation without being surrounded by books and maps and food.

We have packed our thirteen-foot, tow-behind camper with more food, our clothes, our bedding and other accoutrements. The camper is a little, white fiber-glass thing with a rounded shape that looks like an upside-down bathtub, according to our daughter, Barb. She has repeatedly declared: "I could never stay in that thing. I would be claustrophobic!"

Admittedly, the inside is *compact*. Well, maybe *miniscule* would be a better word, but it contains everything we need to live in comfort while traveling. There is a stove top, range-hood complete with fan, sink, refrigerator, furnace, air conditioner, and an electrical convertor. There are beds enough for three not very large people, storage bins galore, a discreetly stored port-a-potty and even a closet, all tucked inside. The walls are carpet-lined which makes the interior fairly quiet. In the roof there is a roll-up screened vent and the side windows have screens and sliding glass. There is even a folding screen door—which one of our dogs managed to open from the outside. We quickly created a bar to put in place to prevent any further unexpected visitors, thanking God it was our own pup and not a raccoon or a skunk that had educated us. The camper is my tiny cabin on wheels: the space I always dreamed of, bigger and sturdier than the long-ago tents, yet small enough to encompass and comfort me.

I am a little over five feet tall. It's the perfect size for me. Jon, at six feet, sort of folds himself into the camper, but he never complains and we have learned to navigate the space well together, as long as he stays seated at the table while I cook, clean up, or otherwise need to occupy floor space!

We bought it the year Jon retired, 1994. In order to make it our own, I had purchased a roll of southwestern patterned wallpaper border and glued it to every flat space I could manage to glue it to. That year we traveled out west, towing the camper behind our Dodge Caravan minivan. We had stopped in Denver to see if I could obtain a copy of my original birth certificate. I even had papers from the judge in Warren. But they were not the right papers. It had been another dead end. But we had a good trip anyway, going on to Colorado Springs and Yellowstone. Along the way we had a little plaque made for the door that read: *ERICKSON'S BED AND BREAKFAST.*

I am comforted that we will be staying in the camper in Lexington where at last I will meet the sister who they say looks just like me.

I called her the week before we left home and to tell her we will be in Lexington, camping at the Kentucky Horse Farm. She has reluctantly agreed to a meeting. We'll meet by the Visitor Registration building of the Farm.

Jon and I are there early, both of us feeling nervous. I am fearful that Ginny might not show up or that she won't like me. Jon is nervous for me, knowing how important this meeting is to me.

We wait and wait. Jon absentmindedly tosses away a cigarette that he's been smoking. There are containers around the grounds for cigarettes. Jon hasn't bothered to use one. I smell something burning and turn to see the still smoldering cigarette has started a fire in some dry mulch. We both stomp on the little fire and scatter the mulch, trying to hide the scorched bits. While we work frantically to hide his crime, a man and woman come up to us.

"Becky?" the woman asks.

"Yes," I answer nervously, looking to see, wondering if this might possibly be my "twin", but she doesn't look as I pictured her. I have short hair, hers is mid-length. I have brown eyes, hers are blue. We are, however, about the same height and build.

"Oh, my gosh!" she exclaims, "I have refused to believe you are my sister. But you look just like Mom! Everyone has always said *I* look like Mom but *you look more like her than I do*. I guess I can't deny you any longer."

We hug but it is a reserved hug. I expected that *she* would feel awkward but suddenly *I* am feeling shy and unsure of myself. We introduce our respective husbands.

"Darrell, Jon—Jon, Darrell."

The four of us decide to walk the grounds. Ginny and I set the pace, walking together and talking. The husbands follow behind searching for any common denominator that will enable them to converse as they trail along behind us, forgotten observers.

We walk around the park. As we walk, we join hands. And I know I have found my "twin". She is not a twin born at the same time as I but the twin of my heart. We are not exact copies of one another but rather more like mirror images. I am a leftie, she is right-handed. I like to sing and while I am no soloist, I can manage to get by in a choir or even in a smaller group. Ginny claims she can't sing. Ginny loves to dance. I was born with two left feet and they aren't even coordinated! I only dance in the privacy of my home if no one else is there. We soon discover we both get grumpy when we are hungry or tired and impossible if we are both! We went to different elementary schools, but to the same junior and senior high schools, had some of the same teachers and many of the same memories of times and places in Warren.

She and Darrell invite us to go to their condo with them. We do. I ask permission to use the bathroom and am astonished to see not only does she have pink bath towels, but they are the same brand as the pink bath towels which hang in our bathroom at home.

But this isn't the first thing we have done alike. We both sent our brother David the same birthday card back in April—mine was bought and mailed from Warren, hers from Lexington. I am thrilled; convinced I have finally found that missing piece—my (almost) twin.

The main difference in us is, I desperately want her in my life and she is not at all certain she wants to have me in hers. Of course, she is too polite to say so, but it is not hard for me to feel the reserve in her manner despite the fact that we have had several spontaneous sessions of the giggles.

Never-the-less, we have a nice day and she and her husband agree to come to Warren for a July 4th family reunion to be held at our home. Ginny has not been with her brothers and sister since her mother's funeral in March of 1989. It is time for the family to reunite.

I can't wait for the Fourth of July to come.

Jon and I make plans, working to get our patio covered before the big day in case of rain. Donna and I work on the logistics. Our kids are all involved. There is excitement in the air. Finally, the day arrives.

It is sunny and hot. The kitchen is filled with women falling over one another trying to be helpful. The men all congregate around the barbeque grill to advise Jon on the best grilling techniques.

Our large "upper yard," located across a stream and connected to the back yard by two foot-bridges becomes a field of dreams for the kids. There is a pick-up softball game, a volley ball net and a proper volley ball bought just for the occasion. There is whiffle ball golf, and even a croquet game going on at various times during the day.

And we take pictures. Family pictures. And I am in them—the missing middle child. I dearly love my adopted brother and sister but I am short and they are tall and we don't have the same sense of humor, but here are people just like me! We laugh at the dumbest things and tell stupid *punny* jokes and have passion for just about everything. We hug a lot and laugh even more.

They are glad to be reunited with one another and they make me feel as though I belong. I sense no resentment about my presence. I feel like the lost piece of a jigsaw puzzle that has finally found its place.

The next day, Norton Sr., the father of my siblings and the man who is named as my father on my birth certificate, invites us all to dinner at a local club. He graciously includes me as part of his kids. All the siblings agree to go. Even though their past with their father has been rugged, like so many abused children, they long for his love and approval. And they want for all of us to be a family. At the club, Ginny and I sit next to one another and talk more. My heart is so full I don't think I can contain one more blessing.

Then it's time for Ginny and her husband to head back to Kentucky. I tell her how wonderfully whole I feel now that I had found her. Little do I know how short lived our relationship will be.

20

On My Own

The following summer, 1997, Jon's brother, Dan, is scheduled to have eye surgery in California where he lives. Dan is a bachelor and Jon wants to be with him for the surgery.

We decide to take the camper and park it on the Outer Banks for a month. Jon will fly out of Norfolk the week after our arrival at Hatteras. I will stay alone for the two-weeks he's gone. He will join me again for the final week of my month at the shore.

Although I have sometimes had my own room, I have never lived alone for a single moment of my life—not even stayed over-night alone. I have gone from Mom's house, to the nursing school dorm, to marrying Jon and living with him. Even when he traveled, I had the kids and my Aunt Evelyn or Jon's dad, Emil living with us.

Staying alone while Jon is gone is my idea. I love the shore, the sound of the surf, the smell of salt and fish and the tang of sea air, the feel of sand between my toes. Jon has asked me repeatedly if I am sure this is what I want to do. I reassure him, I do!

I do. I want to be at the shore for a month. I am even looking forward to some time alone. My mind is overwhelmed with all I have been through, my spirit overwrought and exhausted. I will write. I will write to save my sanity. I will put on paper everything that roars inside of me so I have room for other things.

I read somewhere, or maybe I made it up myself: *A journal is like the key to an airport locker.* When you go on a trip, there are many things you must take with you; clothing, toiletries, important papers, umbrella, camera. There seems to be no end to the stuff that encumbers the traveler. Yet, when one wants to go sightseeing, one does not try to carry all that stuff with them. Oh, it is all important—too important to throw out. So, a wise person rents a locker at the airport and puts all that stuff inside then takes only the key and perhaps their camera with them, freeing them to enjoy the scenery.

The journal is the locker—all the stuff of life; the memories, the hurts, the doubts and fears, the weighty burdens are written down where they will not be forgotten. They are put away safely in a place from which they can be retrieved—in the journal. Then the life traveler is able to move freely, knowing they will never forget even though they no longer carry the experiences of their lives actively in their minds. I need *a locker* in which to put all this stuff. Suspecting I will need more than one locker, I have purchased *several notebooks* and a *big supply* of pens.

As part of my preparation for the trip, I investigate a number of campgrounds. The one we settle on is in Waves, North Carolina, not far from Cape Hatteras. When I phone to make reservations, I anxiously admit that I'll be staying alone while Jon is in California and that I have never in my life stayed alone. I even confess to the fact that I am fifty-two years old. I'm that nervous.

The campground is owned and run by a couple who live in a house right on the grounds. The wife, with whom I speak, seems understanding. She promises to give me a space between two big motor homes owned by folks who are *regulars* and who, she reassures me, will look out for me.

Now the day has come. We have arrived. The kindly couple has checked us in and sent us to the *safe space.*

Jon unhooks the camper from the car, hooks up the electric and water and helps me set up a screen house. The plan is that the screen house will give me some protected outdoor living space. I put a table cloth on the picnic table we have ensconced within its canvas and netting and string some clothes lines with visions of drying towels and having picnics all free from bugs and rain.

Together we explore the area, finding nearby restaurants and shopping places and a little church I plan to attend. *I know I will be OK as long as I have a church.*

I make sure to find the closest pay phone. It will be my lifeline to family and friends while I'm on my own. (It will be many years before I own a cell phone.)

Our children have the number for the campground office so they can call and have us notified if there is an emergency at home. I will check in with them and with Jon on a regular basis.

I am all set to be *on my own* in the little camper.

Our week together flies by and soon it is the day Jon is to fly out. He drives our car to the airport at Norfolk. We are in the unloading lane. He gets out of the car, and I slide into the driver's seat. There is no time for prolonged goodbyes. He kisses me and waves me off to drive back to Hatteras—on my own.

"Be careful, have fun, you'll do fine," I hear him yell as I am forced by traffic to drive away.

Not only have I never *lived* alone, I have never *driven* alone in a strange place.

As a speaker for Christian Women's Clubs, I've driven many new places; in cities, on interstates, down lanes and alleys, but always with a companion. To add to my anxiousness, I'm going to have to cross an impossibly long bridge—while driving alone! I even hate *riding* on bridges, but there is no other way back to Hatteras and my longed-for solitude at the shore.

I drive and I pray. I pray the fervent prayers of a desperate woman. And I arrive safely back at the campground, shaken but sound, vowing I will leave the car in its parking place until I have to go back to Norfolk in two weeks to fetch Jon. I will simply walk everywhere!

The first day alone is fun. I walk the beach, stop in at the camp store and chat with the kindly proprietress, fix a little supper on the stove in the camper.

I take my supper to the screen-house where I enjoy it while feeling smug with myself for being on my own.

Then it gets dark. The bathhouse, which by daylight was just across the way, seems to have moved, the path longer than I remembered. I take my flashlight and march forth. When I return, I securely lock the screen door with the stick through the handles and the inside door with the lock that must have a key to open from the outside. I am snug in my "upside down bathtub."

I tuck myself into my bed that is the sofa by day. One end of the camper has the table that makes into a double bed and the other end of the camper—a whole six feet away—has a narrow sofa built over the storage bins. As long as I'm going to be alone, I decide there's no need to lower the table and make it into a bed each night. I will sleep on the sofa, tucked in next to the stove, under the rear window where I can open the curtain and look into the night sky once I'm settled in. I put my weary, excited self to bed.

Then my eyes, so heavy with sleep, pop open, and seem determined to stay that way throughout the long, dark night that is suddenly filled with strange rustlings and the deep roar of the surf booming against the shore.

Eventually, I do sleep and sometime in the night, a Nor'easter arrives.

I awaken in the morning to find my little home rocking in the moaning wind. Instead of the gentle lap of waves, I hear the surf pounding and suddenly I'm grateful to be behind a dune and between two substantial campers. As I open the door to greet the day, the wind grabs it, nearly tearing it off the hinges. I'm not too worried. Nor'easters blow themselves out fairly quickly in May.

I fix my solitary breakfast, bundle up, take a notebook, a pen and the bright orange whistle someone told me I should have if I am going to be a *woman alone on the beach,* and set off for the thundering shore. As I head up over the dunes, the fierceness of the wind takes me by surprise, nearly knocking me off my feet.

I struggle along the surf's edge, making sure I'm headed into the wind so I will have it at my back when I return, reassuring myself I'll enough energy to get home. After a half hour, I turn around, in five minutes I find I'm back at the dune where I began.

OK! I guess that will have to do for today, I decide and climb the dune where I find a small cranny in the sand just big enough for me. I curl up, take out my notebook and began to write; about finding my family, about the disconnected feeling that comes from growing up Rebecca Samuelson and finding out I am also Sharon Bennod. I write and my writing feels like my soul is retching, bringing information and pain from the deepest recesses of my being. I write about brothers and sisters—adopted and biological (or half-biological?). I write my battered heart onto that paper and soak it with tears. When I can bear no more, I return to the camper for a nap.

And thus, go my days, one following the other. Each morning I check in with the campground owners and have a nice chat, then walk to the pay phone and call home to be sure all was well there. I struggle up the beach and blow back and climb into my sandy lair and write. That takes care of my mornings but I'm lonely. Jon is three hours behind us in time and busy with caring for his brother. He has told me which evenings he will call. The continent that separates us is wide.

One morning, I decide to try calling Ginny even though I am pretty sure she is working. I just want to hear her voice. I *need her.* The phone rings and rings. I imagine it resounding through their empty condo. Then she answers.

"Ginny, it's Becky. I was afraid you would be at work. But here you are! You're not sick, are you?"

"Becky! No, I'm not sick, but Darrell just had heart surgery. I don't know if he is going to make it. I can't believe you called. I just came home to shower and get some clean clothes. I am so glad to hear your voice. I am scared, Sis."

We talk and talk. I feel so close to her. I promise to be praying for both of them and to call again in a couple of days. I hang up the phone, my heart filled with love for my *almost twin.*

I return to my little home to find that directly across the road from my camp site two young men have pitched a tent. I suppose they've come planning on a few fun-in-the-sun days on the beach but we're still in the midst of the Nor'easter. They don't seem to know what to do in the constant howling storm. Like me, they try to walk the beach and return windblown and exhausted and crawl into their tent to escape the blasting sand and moaning wind.

One of them, the younger one, speaks to me when we meet on the road. He has blonde hair, blue eyes, and an innocent open face. He notices that my screen house has taken a beating in the wind. One of the corner posts has broken causing the whole structure to kneel, like a camel waiting to be mounted.

"I would be glad to help you with your screen house," he offers each time we meet.

"Thank you very much," I reply, "but I don't think there is any point in trying to fix it while the wind is so fierce."

"OK," he says, "but don't forget I will be glad to help you."

We never need new words. These words are sufficient, day after day.

I can't help but notice the two men struggle to cook over a tiny campfire that's barely able to hold its own against the relentless winds. There's a restaurant within close walking distance that serves shrimp for ten cents apiece during happy hour. I eat there often, adding a salad and a beverage to my 10 ten cent shrimp to create a full meal for under $5! I figure my young neighbors are probably on a tight budget like I am, so one day I take my coffee cup and walk over to their tent.

They are in their tent, but I call out, "Hi," feeling quite comfortable about my visit considering the kindness of the young man who daily offers to help me with the screen house.

The older of the two men crawls out of the tent. He has a dark countenance, his eyes glow yellow like those of a predatory cat. He's not pleased to see me.

"Um, I just noticed you struggling to cook over a campfire in this horrible wind and I thought I would let you know that the restaurant right near here has ten cent shrimp for happy hour," I stammer, suddenly nervous.

"Yeah, I know. We're not interested," he growls and turning his back on me reenters the tent.

I feel stupid and a little threatened. I quickly return to the safety of the little camper.

That night, I don't open my curtain to watch the night sky. I am uncomfortable about the men in the tent across the way. I toss and turn on my narrow sofa bed. I get up and check the lock on the door.

Morning finally arrives but I don't open my curtain and greet the morning. A deep foreboding has overtaken me. A feeling of terror rises in my throat making it hard to breathe.

"Becky, this is silly!" I admonish myself sternly but I can't shake this fear. So, I do the only thing I can think to do. I begin to sing the doxology. "Praise God from whom all blessings flow. Praise Him all creatures here below." I sing in a loud voice as bravely as I can. "Praise Him above ye heavenly host; praise Father, Son, and Holy Ghost." I sing over and over until I feel calmer. But my bowels are twisting and cramping. I won't use the port-a-potty for this so I timidly open my door and walk the path to the bathhouse, one eye on *their* campsite. No one appears to be stirring.

I don't stay long. Just long enough to answer the call of nature and brush my teeth. I just want to be back in the camper, tucked between the two substantial motor homes, each of which has a big, friendly man and wife within.

When I come out of the bathhouse, I am astonished to see the tent is gone. There's no evidence it has ever been there. There's no evidence of a fire having burned in the fire ring. The clothesline that was between the trees at their campsite is gone. There's no trash anywhere. The grass is not compacted. It's as though they were never there at all.

As I look at that pristine site, the hair on my arms stands on end. I shiver. *What did I come in contact with?* I wonder. Whatever it was, I believe singing the doxology over and over was my saving grace. We have tented for years. I know it's *not humanly possible* for that tent to be gone and the site look untouched after those two men had been there for four days—all in a time of less than 10 minutes.

(As I have reflected on that event over the years, I have wondered if the older man had some awful power over the younger one. Was the younger man reaching out to me for help? I have no idea but I have prayed all these years for those two—especially that open-faced almost child man who offered so faithfully to help me with my screen house.)

108

The rest of the time I am encamped there, I never have another uneasy moment.

The campground lady and I have struck up a sort of friendship over my daily visits. She invites me to see their house—they just bought a new sleigh bed and she's very excited. A few evenings she has joined me for happy hour and ten cent shrimp across the road.

One day she knocks at the camper door.

"Becky," she calls, "Your daughter, Barb, called. She wants you to call her back."

In a panic, I rush out the door nearly knocking her over. I forget to say, "Thank you."

I run to the payphone and call Barb. "Is everything ok?"

"It's all fine, Mom," she reassures me. "I know you are down there to spend time alone and to write but I was just wondering if I could possibly fly down and spend a week with you before Dad gets back? It's ok if you don't want me to...I understand."

I am relieved and astonished.

"But, Barb, I am living in *the upside-down bathtub* that you could never stand to be in," I remind her a bit gleefully.

I know how she loves the ocean. I know it has taken a lot of courage for her to ask to come but I am so relieved there is no bad news that I can't resist teasing her.

"I know. I knew you would say that! But...I shouldn't have asked. I'm sorry."

I have to think about this. Do I really want to share my solitude? My little camper? My first taste of "living alone?" I think only a minute. I would love to have her company.

"Honey, I would love to have you," I reply.

I know the week we spend will be a special, a once in a lifetime experience. Barb is married, working, busy, and no longer *my little girl.* Now she's a woman, like me.

"I just have to warn you, I need about 3 hours of quiet time on the dune every morning. I have to get this stuff out of my system and writing is so healing."

"Mom, I won't say a word," she promises. I know she can keep that promise. We have always been able to be together without talking and be comfortable.

After I hang up the phone, I realize I'm going to have to get in my car, drive across *that bridge*, drive to the airport in Norfolk and drive back again to fulfill the wishes of my daughter. But I learned long ago, a mom can and will do anything for her children. I have a couple of days to pray about it and prepare for my "house guest."

I call Ginny to tell her the news and she tells me she has just brought Darrell home from the hospital. They put stents in his heart. She is furious with him because on the way home he insisted she stop at a fast food place so he could get a giant burger and an extra-large fries.

I understand her fury. Darrell has no idea the worry his condition has caused nor does he seem to care that his behavior is not going to help his health. We commiserate. I promise to call again soon.

I do. She never answers.

Barb arrives. The Nor'easter stays and stays and stays. Each morning, we struggle up the beach together and blow back; our 35-minute exhausting beach walk. Then one day, we find we have walked all the way to the pier, a pier nearly a mile away that we haven't even been able to see before and it takes just as long to walk back as it took to walk up.

The Nor'easter's finally gone, and when it blows itself out to sea, I read in the local paper that this Nor'easter had broken all records since 1907. They are calling it the Winter of June.

Two days after the Nor'easter has gone, I drive once more to Norfolk airport, this time to return Barb and to pick up Jon.

Jon drives back to the campground. When we get back, he compliments me on my new dolphin earrings. I explain to him they were bought in celebration of my new-found bravery: "I stayed alone for a week before Barb came and God protected me from evil. And, I drove back and forth across that long bridge and navigated my way to the airport *twice*. I have much to celebrate."

Jon agrees, pleased that I have made these huge steps toward independence.

The earrings become a talisman reminding me of these events through a lot of braver events to come.

My three weeks of cathartic writing are over.

The last week at the shore, Jon and I walk, wade in the now calm Atlantic waters, read on the beach, eat out and just enjoy being together.

Life is good.

21

Then He Left Me

No matter how hard I have tried to fight it, God has a calling on my life that has left me exhausted and confused.

In April, 1998, I decide that I will spend 40 Days in the Wilderness—by journaling for 40 days while seeking to discern what that call is. I figure Moses spent 40 years in the desert as a shepherd before God called him to lead the people out of Egypt but I am rather too old to wait 40 more years. Jesus spent 40 days in the wilderness before beginning his ministry. That seems more reasonable at my age.

I go out and buy a new journal to be dedicated solely to this process and I begin. Every day I, like Jacob, wrestle with the Lord, but he doesn't enlighten me. Still, I won't let go. I miss some days. I am even tempted to give the whole notion up but I persevere. The "40 Days" becomes nearly three months but even with my procrastination, eventually I arrive at day 39. I still don't know for sure but I have a strong suspicion, so I don't write for a day or two, avoiding the 40th day as long as I dare. Finally, I sit in the red rocker, the chair we bought when Kristina was born so many years ago, and find myself writing, "There is no doubt. God is calling me to be a pastor."

I am overwhelmed with a sense of relief that the issue is finally settled. I get out of my chair and fall on my knees in a prayer of praise. Tears stream down my face. I have finally come to the end of my struggle and then it hits me: *I can't be a pastor! What is God thinking? I am too old. I am too uneducated. I am too poor. And I am a woman!* I immediately inform God of all these very obvious things. But He doesn't seem to care very much about my opinion.

After considerable thought, I decide that if I become a lay-pastor, God will settle down and be satisfied. It is the obvious solution.

In a few days I work up my courage and make an appointment to meet with our pastor, Glenn Hamilton.

"Glenn," I say, once I am seated in his office, "I have been struggling with this for some time and I think maybe God is calling me to be a pastor. I was wondering what you think and if maybe I could become a lay-pastor."

Much to my horror, Glenn laughs. It is not a polite snicker. It is a deep belly laugh.

When he has finally gotten himself under control, he shakes his head and says, "I have been waiting for you. I have known God has a call on your life for some time. I wondered how long it would be before you showed up here."

I don't know whether to be relieved or terrified. I am a bit of both. We spend the next hour going over what I will need to do in order to apply for a lay-pastor's license with the Covenant. I arrive home with papers to be filled out and a trembling heart.

Glenn has far more confidence in my Biblical knowledge than I do. I know there is so much I don't know. I learn of a correspondence course at Moody Bible Institute and while I have no idea how I will pay for it, I send for the information. Our finances are tight and I am both prideful and stubborn. I determine that I won't take the money from our household accounts to pay for the course even though Jon insists that I should. Then my step-father calls us kids together and surprises each of us; Debbie, Jim and me with a gift of money. It is Mom's life insurance. We protest but he insists that we accept it. It's enough to begin my studies.

I order the first course Moody requires, an overview of the Bible, and begin a walk that will take me beyond anything I could have ever imagined or dreamed of in my wildest dreams.

I apply for and am granted my lay-license. The Moody course arrives. I devour it and then the next one and the next. I am also studying from the books on the lay-pastors' required reading list. I can't seem to get enough or learn it fast enough. I am like a starving person being offered food.

Glenn invites me to attend a group of pastors that meet early on Friday mornings for Bible study and prayer at the First United Methodist Church in Warren. I want to go but despite the fact I have been a public speaker for years, I am shy in small groups of people I don't know. Not only do I not know these people but I am not even sure they will welcome me. After all, I know that every pastor there is a man and an ordained minister.

They come from many different denominations, although two of them are Covenant pastors. There are about 20 when they are all in attendance. They have been together for a long time. Although sometimes the individuals change with pastors going off to new calls and others coming to take their place, it is a cohesive group.

Friday morning, I get up at 6 AM and shower. I put on slacks and a blouse. *No*, I decide, *too casual.* I slip into a dress, but that seems too formal. I finally settle for a skirt and jacket with a simple shell underneath. There is no more time. I want to stay home but Glenn has promised to meet me in the parking lot. I have to go.

When I get to the church, I realize I don't know where the parking lot for the church is. Well, I know it is in the back but I am not sure how to access it. I find a driveway marked exit but no one is exiting and it is getting late so I quickly drive in and to my relief see Glenn's car.

The pastors look startled when we enter together. Glenn introduces me and they welcome me because it was *the Christian thing to do* and because Glenn had brought me. I know I am blessed to have a pastor who believes in women's rights to pursue their God-given calling, whatever it might be.

We drink coffee and eat donuts and I find they are funny and fun and most of them are dressed in jeans and sweatshirts. There is a lot of punning going on—and I jump right in but *the guys,* as they call themselves, are patronizing toward me.

As we leave, Glenn apologizes. Their patronizing behavior annoys Glenn no end but I assure him it doesn't annoy me, and in time I believe I can win them over.

I return the next week and the next and soon I seem to fit right in. They have stopped saying *"you guys and lady, of course"* after I assure them I don't mind being one of *the guys.* However, one pastor has left the group. He was always sharing stories about the things God would tell him to do, including how to fix his truck. His comfortable yet reverent relationship with the Lord is the kind of relationship we all long to have and we all miss him. Several members of the group call him to tell him so, but he stays away for several months.

Much to everyone's delight, one Friday morning, he returns.

"I have a confession to make," he says when our time of drinking coffee, dunking donuts, and punning our way to wakefulness is over. "I left because I didn't think it was right for a woman to be in ministry." He looks at me with a gentle expression. "As I have been seeking the Lord in prayer over these weeks, He has shown me that I was wrong. I am glad He was patient with me and I am glad to be back. And I am very glad Becky is with us."

Tears threaten to overtake me. I notice I am not alone in pulling out a tissue.

The weeks became months. The months soon add up to nearly two years. With my lay-license, I am able to help with the ministry at the church and even to attend Covenant pastors' retreats. I am continually studying and I want more.

In the fall of 1998, Jon and I attend a Pastor and Spouse Fall Retreat. The recruiter from the seminary is seated at the table where Jon, Pastor Glenn, and I are eating. He turns to Jon, assuming Jon is the pastor of our couple and asks, "Do you know of any young people we should be recruiting for seminary?"

Jon doesn't reply. He just looks at the recruiter, a young man named Mark, with a puzzled expression.

Glenn, who recognizes Mark's presumption, shakes his head. "Mark, you have a lot to learn. Jon is not the pastor, Becky is. And we think *she* should be going to seminary, so when you get your foot out of your mouth, you need to talk to her."

Jon's quick to agree.

I'm in shock. Seminary? Surely not seminary. After all, I know I am too old. I have no undergraduate degree—in fact I am still struggling to get an Associate's Degree in Bible Studies with the Moody correspondence course. I'm not struggling with grades but struggling to find the time to study and learn everything that I want to learn. I have no money. And I am a woman.

That evening, Mark finds me and apologizes for assuming Jon is the pastor. He hands me an application to North Park Theological Seminary in Chicago. I quickly set him straight as to why it is impossible for me to even consider attending seminary.

Now it's his turn to laugh. "Becky," he says, "We have no age limits. We are legally permitted to take up to 10% of the class from the *school of life*. We have grants and loans for students. And we accept women! I will be waiting for you to submit this. Oh, and as proof of your ability to do the academic work, attach one or two of your Moody papers and your grades to date. I understand from Glenn that you are a very good and dedicated student."

I take the papers home, put them on the desk in my office and ignore them as best I can, but it seems to me that every time I go into the office the papers rustle, demanding my attention. I struggle in prayer. I ask *the guys* at the Friday morning Bible Study to be praying for me and with me. They all encourage me to fill out the papers. Eventually, I do.

I will fill these out, mail them in, they will reject me and that will be the end of this nonsense.

Winter comes, seems to last forever, and is on the way out and I still haven't heard from the seminary one way or the other. One day, as I am shopping at the mall, I see a down jacket with a hood trimmed in fur. It is deep purple and fits like it was made for me. Although it weighs next to nothing, when I try it on, it is so warm I can hardly get it off fast enough.

This would be perfect for the Windy City in the winter, but I haven't heard a word from the school so it's silly to even think about needing this.

I take it to the register and pay for it. When I take it home and model it for Jon he says, "That will be perfect for Chicago next winter."

In late May, when the days finally warm in Northwestern Pennsylvania and we are sitting out on the front porch, an envelope arrives from NPTS. I fumble trying to open it. My hands tremble. The envelope drops on the porch floor.

"Do you want me to open it for you?" Jon offers.

"No! I mean, no, thank you. I can do this. I'm just not sure I really want to know."

But I *do* want to know.

I finally manage to extract the letter and read, "We are pleased to notify you that you have been accepted as a student of North Park Theological Seminary..."

Stunned, I merely nod.

Jon whoops with joy. "I knew it! I told you. I am so excited for you and so proud of you."

I burst into tears, overwhelmed by the knowing, without really knowing, that our lives have forever been changed.

There is so much to be done. In June, our daughter, Barb, and I make a trip to the school so I can choose an apartment in student housing. While it will be more expensive for me to have my own apartment than to have a roommate, I know if I am going to survive, having my own place is critical. Together we measure the rooms, make drawings of each noting where windows and doors and radiators are located.

When we got home, we will figure what furniture I will bring and where each piece will be placed and every picture hung. It comforts me to know we have planned this together.

I pack. I unpack. I repack. Jon rents a U-Haul van. The week of August 23, 1999, we head for Chicago. Jon's friend, Dan, follows in his car. They will leave the van in Chicago after it is empty and drive home together. Jon's business and his father will keep him in Warren while God's business and my Father will keep me in Chicago.

It was just two years ago I stayed alone for the first time in the little camper at the shore. Now I will be living alone in Chicago. I am 54 years old.

The men unload my stuff from the van and place each thing according to the scale drawings Barb and I have made. We go to a nearby restaurant for dinner then find the U Haul place and leave the empty van. The men stay the night. Dan sleeps in the single bed in my bedroom. Jon and I share the futon in the living room. I cling to him hoping morning will never come, but it does.

After making sure I have food to eat and am as settled as I can be, Jon kisses me goodbye and we hold each other in a desperate way. Finally, he and Dan go out the door and get into Dan's car.

I stand looking out the dirty little window over the kitchen table watching my husband and his friend drive away. I can't believe he left me, he actually left me!

My heart pounds pushing itself up through my chest and filling my throat. My head spins. I tremble, drenched in sweat.

I know I am going to die.

It makes no sense to die on the kitchen table. I decide I will go lie on the bed to die.

Forcing my mushy knees and liquid legs forward, I go to the bedroom.

I lie on the bed breathing the ragged breath of terror. I wait to die.

I wait to die.

But I do not die.

I remember when Jesus raised a little girl from the dead, he told her parents to feed her. It seems practical advice.

I drag myself from the bed and stagger to the kitchen.

Opening the refrigerator, I scan the food we had bought the day before. Bile rises, its bitter acid burning my throat. There is nothing I will not vomit out as soon as it goes in. I am about to close the door when a flash of red catches my eye. There on the back of the top shelf is a piece of watermelon.

I take it out, remembering how years before my mother-in-law told me that after a long bout of stomach flu, watermelon was the only thing she could keep down.

I lift it from the coolness of the refrigerator and gaze at the plate on which it sits. The plate, a piece of hand painted china brought from home, pale green covered in pink dogwood flowers, comforts.

I pick up the watermelon, bite into its cold, crunchy, red interior. The sweet juice drips from my chin mixing with the salty tears flowing down my cheeks.

I will live to see another day. After all, I *am* wearing my dolphin earrings.

22

Pastor Becky

Wanting to have plenty of time to settle my apartment and explore the area, I have arrived in Chicago several days before classes are to begin. It seemed such a good idea at the time but now I look around and can't think of anything I want to do. And I am terrified to even go outdoors, much less go exploring. It takes me two days to get brave enough to leave my porch, walk down my back stairs and onto the street.

Whatever made me think I could do this? I am a country girl. I am afraid of everything. I am out of my element in every way. O Lord, if this is truly your doing—I need help!

I manage to get to the restaurant where Jon and I have eaten before. *Georges* is a Greek restaurant directly across Foster Ave. from the campus. George and Ellen Sovakis own the restaurant; he cooks, she waits table. They work hard and they love the North Park students, welcoming them with open arms and hearts. They have already promised Jon they will keep an eye on me. When I walk in the door, Ellen calls out "Becky, come sit. I'm just taking a break." Ellen is a little older than I am but right from the start, she feels more like a sister than a new acquaintance. Little do I know, Ellen and George will be key to my staying in school—feeding me, mopping up my tears, encouraging me when I am sure I can't stay one more minute, and becoming life-long friends.

I start a new journal thinking that one day I will write a book about my seminary years. I do this without knowing that I will be too overwhelmed, exhausted and stretched for time to write much of anything in the journal. I will have to trust pictures, memories, friends, and papers if I am ever going to write the book—but I do have a title, Too Old, Too Poor, Too Uneducated! And now I can add: Too scared! Besides, I am fairly certain I will never live to see graduation or even survive to the end of the first semester.

On August 29, after what seems an eternity but is only a few days, the day has come for Convocation, the official start of seminary. We students have been given a sheaf of papers and among them is one with instructions for Convocation. IT IS MANDATORY. No student will be permitted to skip Convocation. The hours drag. I take a bath and do my hair and put on my very favorite dress. It is a long Mandarin-style dress of dark red with black woven through it. When I wear it, I always feel confident that I am well dressed. I look at the clock once again. Time drags. Finally, I set off for Nyvall Hall where the Convocation is being held in the chapel. When I arrive the door of the chapel opens and people come streaming out.

Someone takes my arm and says, "You are staying for refreshments, aren't you? We need to go this way."

I am horrified. I am an hour late. Somehow, I got my times confused. I have missed the mandatory Convocation. I am sick with panic sure they will tell me I will have to leave seeing I couldn't even be trusted to attend the first event of my education. I try to mingle, hoping my distinct dress will imprint my presence on the instructors and deans and they will assume I was actually inside for the service. I nibble at the edges of the hors d'oeuvres on my paper plate and fight the urge to vomit. As soon as I am able, I flee to my apartment and fling myself onto my bed crying with shame and fear.

I just need to talk with Ginny. O God, please, I need to talk with my sister. She will understand.

I look up her number in my address book and dial all the numbers on my phone card and finally, at the prompt, her number. The phone rings and rings on the other end. Ginny hasn't answered any of my calls for months.

Just as I am ready to hang up, she answers.

"Oh, Sis," I wail, "I think I am going to be kicked out of seminary."

"Becky? What on earth are you talking about? Donna told me you just got there. What terrible thing could you have done?" she asks, her voice completely bewildered.

"I missed my Convocation—and it was mandatory. I thought it started at 3 and I waited and waited to go but 3 was the time of the reception. The service was at 2. How am I going to do this when I can't even get the only thing I have been given to do right?"

"Now listen, Sister. I am sure they are not going to kick you out because you missed Convocation. Besides if you were at the reception, they probably think you were at the whole thing. How many students are there? Like only 10?"

"No," I reply, "I don't know how many but there were a lot."

"Well, there, you see. It will be fine. Now go wash your face and make some coffee."

I follow her advice and pretend I know what the speaker said when the Convocation address is spoken of by my classmates. Three years later, I will buy a DVD with the service on it and actually listen to the address I missed that day. It was a good message.

I am absolutely paranoid about all scheduling from that point on. I will record in my day planner every paper due, every test date, every lecture I am to attend. And I will put them on a monthly calendar as well so I can see the big picture. I will review these dates and times with classmates making sure I haven't missed anything. I will create false, early deadlines for everything so papers will actually be done before their due dates. Over time, I become the student everyone else checks with when they are uncertain of anything. I do not miss another deadline. And I have no more chats with my sister. Somehow, I never find her at home again but her voice continues to echo in my head and heart, a steadying force in my chaotic life as a seminary student.

The semesters pass and I continue to hang in there, but living 510 miles apart from Jon is putting a strain on our marriage. My life as a student not only separates us in distance but in virtually every way possible.

Jon comes to spend Thanksgivings with me. I go home for about a month at Christmas. I am home for about three months in the summer but my heart and mind never really leave Chicago. Along with studies, I am working at Evanston Covenant Church with young Chinese and Korean students. I spend a semester doing a study/internship through a program called SCUPE: Seminary Consortium for Urban Pastoral Education. I work at a homeless shelter and fall in love with urban ministry. I have visions of being a minister in Chicago when I graduate but those visions are not shared by Jon.

In the fall of 2001, I know I must return home. I seek counsel from my spiritual directors and the Dean of Students. They confirm that it is time for me to leave seminary proper.

By the end of the semester, I have 80 of the 96 credit hours that I must have to graduate. As for the rest of the credits, I can continue my education with on-line courses, an option that is just in its infancy—directed studies—and returning to Chicago for intensives. Everyone at school wants me to be able to finish. God's calling for me to become an ordained pastor has been affirmed over and over. The biggest challenge will be how to meet my CPE (Clinical Pastoral Education) requirement. There are no hospitals close to Warren that offer CPE but we decide to leave that to be worked out when and how God sees fit.

December, 2001, is filled with papers and finals and packing up my apartment which has been my home in Chicago for the past 2 ½ years. And then it is time.

Jon arrives and rents a tow-behind U Haul. My fellow students help him pack everything in. I take my plants in the car with me so they won't freeze. We leave Chicago. It has been a wonderful experience and I will miss my little home. Although I will be returning for intensive classes, I will no longer have my own place here. I will stay with friends. I leave with both joy and sorrow.

As we leave Chicago behind, I realize that in the years since I have found my family, I have truly found myself. I am no longer afraid of everything. I have learned to navigate Chicago by bus and subway on my own. I have repeatedly taken the train from Erie to Chicago and back. I have completed the majority of my studies with honors. The dolphin earrings have been replaced. My Chinese friends felt sorry for me that I had only one pair of earrings and bought me a pair of cat earrings so I would have some variety. I didn't tell them why I always wore the dolphins. I no longer *need* them although I still treasure them.

We are in the midst of a blizzard by the time we get to Erie. I think we ought to just find a place to stay and wait out the storm but Jon is intent on getting home. Eventually it becomes impossible to see and we are forced to give up. We find a motel that has a room for an astronomical sum of money. Grateful, we take it. At breakfast the next morning we meet our fellow stranded and scalped travelers. It is still impossible to see more than 3 feet when looking out the lobby windows. We all linger, chatting, dressed in sweats suits and fuzzy slippers, grateful for hot coffee and a safe place even though we know we have been taken advantage of. Eventually the wind subsides; the snow plows come through and open roads that were closed just after we got off them. We head out for the last stretch home.

I sit muttering, "Paper or plastic" over and over.

Jon asks "What on earth is the matter with you?"

I tell him it's a joke—a sort of sick joke—among seminary students leaving full time studies. Once we are no longer full-time, we have to begin to repay our student loans and that often means getting a job in a grocery store because it is hard for students to find a job in ministry.

"Besides," I inform him, "I was told by my fellow students that I already have two strikes against me; I am too old and I am a woman."

This was not how I had planned for my life to go, but going it is and I know despite all my desires and disappointments, God is still in charge and I'm doing the right thing. It just feels all wrong.

We arrive at home on a Thursday. The things I took to seminary no longer seem to fit back into the house and of course, there are more things than I started with. We just leave it all in boxes and put everything in the basement. It's time to think about Christmas.

The following Monday I receive a call. A man asks, "Is this Pastor Becky?"

"Yes," I answered tentatively.

"My name is Seth Bloomquist. I am chairman of Emmanuel Mission Church in Kane. Our pastor has resigned and will be leaving the end of this month. One of our members mentioned that you are a seminary student and are going to finish up your education but are going to do it from home. Anyway, we were wondering if maybe you would be interested in being our interim pastor—just until we can find someone permanent. We understand you would have to take time off for classes sometimes but that can be arranged."

I am too astonished to reply. In the moments of silence that follow his offer I think of a thousand things. The first being how much I hate to drive in the winter—and once even vowed that no one on earth could ever make me drive Route 6 east in the winter. Kane is 45 minutes east on Route 6 and this is winter! The second thing I remember is that the current superintendent of the Great Lakes Conference, the one Kane is located in, once told me I should plan to be a chaplain because no church in that conference would ever call a woman pastor. The third thing to cross my mind is that I would be saying, "The Lord bless you and keep you. The Lord make his face to shine on you and give you peace," not "paper or plastic?"

Finally, Seth says, "I know you will want some time to pray about this."

Oh yeah, that should have been number one on my list and I didn't even think of it. Maybe I'm not ready to be a pastor after all.

I agree with Seth that this needs to be a matter of prayerful discernment and discussion with Jon. Seth than adds, "We don't want to rush you but we would appreciate an answer by Friday. If you don't feel called to come, we need to look for someone else."

"Friday? This Friday? Well, yes, of course I can let you know by Friday. I am sure the Lord will make it all clear by Friday—this is only Monday," I babble and then fear they will change their minds for sure because I sound like an idiot.

"Ok, then," Seth says. He is obviously not one for idle chatter. "I will be eager to hear from you. Have a good week. Good bye."

"Yes, you too. And thank you for calling. I'll be in touch soon."

I hang up the phone and go looking for Jon. I will pray but first I need a flesh and blood person to hold me up, my mushy knees have returned.

On my birthday, March 30, 2001, while I was at a SCUPE convention, I had received a powerful anointing for ministry. I can't describe it because I don't have the words to, but I was overwhelmed by the presence of the Holy Spirit. It was as if the Lord spoke to me without words, saying, "You have just begun the second half of your life."

As I was sharing that experience with one of the speakers, a woman pastor with a powerful story, she looked at me and said, "Yes, I can see God dancing in your eyes."

The first Sunday in January, 2002, with Jon at the wheel of our car, we drive to Kane and I begin the second half of my life.

The people are warm and welcoming and incredibly patient with me as I learn the real bricks and mortar of ministry. They decide it would be best if I come to Kane on Saturdays in order to have time to meet the families. They arrange for me to stay at the little motel not far from the church, but soon we decide it would be better if I would use the parsonage next door to the church. I have all the furniture I will need—pictures for the walls even, stored in our basement all boxed up and ready to move. Once again, Jon rents a U Haul, but this time I will only be away from home two nights of the week, Saturday and Wednesday. I drive over on Wednesday mornings, teach a ladies' Bible study, do visitation, teach an evening Bible study and head for home Thursday morning.

By September of 2003, the congregation has decided to issue a call for a permanent position of pastor—to me. There is a new conference superintendent, one who is very supportive of women in ministry, Rev. Richard Lucco, who comes to preside over my installation on October 26, 2003. I am the only solo woman pastor in the conference. Thankfully, over time, that will change.

Once I am properly installed, the board confesses to me they didn't want a woman pastor—no one wanted a woman pastor—but I was their only option and they had agreed they could *put up with me* for a few months until they found the *right pastor.* We all have a good laugh about it and agree only God could have pulled this one off because I had vowed never to drive Route 6

126

east in the winter—*I didn't want them either.*

I love being Pastor Becky. My life is full and mostly happy. I drive Route 6 in the summer, fall, winter and spring, only occasionally cancelling services when the weather is not only unsafe for me to drive to them but for them to drive to church. The parsonage is my second home, an extension of my life in Chicago. I continue to take classes and work toward one day actually graduating from seminary!

But there is a piece of me missing. For reasons I cannot understand and no one can explain to me, Ginny has simply cut off all communication with me. I grieve the loss of "my other half" that I had waited so long to find and now have lost. Every Christmas and birthday and holiday in between, I send her a little card but she doesn't answer. I pray for her and I wait, trusting that in His time, God will bring us together once again.

23

My Bath Towels Are White

The year is 2005. Time seems to go faster and faster. Jon's piano business is busy. My stepfather is failing. Jon's father, who has now been moved to the nursing home close to the church in Kane, is slowing growing weaker.

Ministry is a great joy. It is also an exhausting calling. I am blessed to be close to all my siblings, both my adopted ones and the new ones, and we are in constant contact, all but Ginny, that is. Donna, David and Norrie have reassured me it is nothing I have done, that it is just Ginny, but it grieves me. May 20 is Ginny's birthday, so I buy a card and write a little note, just as I have done for the past six years, always hoping that maybe this will be the one to move her to contact me. I mail it early, making sure it won't be late. I want my sister to know I have not forgotten her—I will never forget her.

Jon and I desperately need time away, time alone, time to rest and recuperate. We make reservations to spend a week at Cape Hatteras on the Outer Banks the week leading into Memorial Day, our forty-second wedding anniversary.

We leave home early in the morning on Friday, May 20. We don't rush. We stay overnight in Virginia and arrive at our motel in Buxton on Saturday. After unpacking the car and hauling everything to our second-floor efficiency apartment, with balcony overlooking the Atlantic Ocean, we go out to eat. The evening is peaceful. The ocean surf takes me back to my weeks in the little camper in a campground not far from where we are staying now. It is the first time in a long time I feel really at peace.

Then my cell phone rings. I answer.

"Ma baath tauls aw whaat," a woman with a Southern accent informs me.

"I beg your pardon?" I ask.

"Ma baath tauls aw whaat."

"Who is calling?" I can't imagine who this is or what on earth this woman wants. I figure it's a wrong number.

"It's your sister, Ginny, and ma baath tauls aw whaat."

As soon as she said "Sister Ginny", I knew what she was talking about. In that little note I had sent with her birthday card I had written, "It is hard to believe we first met ten years ago. Back then we both had pink bath towels, mine are navy now, what color are yours?" I had also included both our home and my cell phone number. When I sent the note, it seemed stupid to talk about bath towels with a sister who hasn't spoken to me since August of 1999, the day of my convocation crisis, but my sister tells me that it was that one little line that touched her so deeply she just had to call.

My sister is back! O Lord, thank you! Thank you! What a perfect beginning to our vacation.

Sunday morning, I find a church and attend the worship. The service is at 10 AM. Jon has chosen not to join me but I am comfortable alone. The congregation is small and friendly. I return to our apartment. At noon, I get another call on my cell phone and this time I know it is Ginny because I have put her name and number into my contacts.

A terrible tragedy has just happened and she says, "You were the only one I could think to call." Her soon to be son-in-law had just been killed in a motorcycle accident.

My phone number was the last one she had called from her cell phone. She only had to hit redial. We talk for an hour, cry together for the terrible loss that has happened in the past couple of hours, and pray together.

She tells me she is sorry it has taken her so long to call me. I tell her I understand it's a lot to process and I've known about her long before she knew about me. Before we hang up, we say together, "I love you."

Lord, thank you for white bath towels, silly notes, and your perfect timing. I grieve for my sister's heart ache. I thank you she has let me help her bear it. I know we will be OK.

And it is OK. Ginny and I talk often. She has explained that when we first met it was exciting but as time went along, she became more and more confused and even angry. She said it was as though she had suddenly grown a third leg and didn't know how to understand such a thing happening much less know how to walk with it. We get together whenever we can although it isn't easy because she and her husband run a very successful cleaning business and it is hard for her to get away. But we dream of the day we will live closer to one another and are able to do things together and it would sure be nice if we lived in some place warm!

24

Epilogue

How the years have flown. I can't believe it is 2020 already and I have been retired since November 30, 2010, after serving nine years at Emmanuel Mission Covenant Church in Kane.

I had planned to stay longer. After all, I didn't actually graduate from seminary until May 2006 and was finally formally ordained at the Annual Meeting of the Evangelical Covenant Church of America in Portland, Oregon on June 24, 2007. But, early summer of 2010, I began to run fevers and my body ached in every bone, muscle and nerve. My doctor ran test after test trying to determine what was wrong. Finally, by divine inspiration, I am sure, he tested me for mononucleosis. The test came back positive. I was teased mercilessly about getting "teenage kissing disease" but there is nothing funny about having mono when you are 65 years old. I lived from one mega dose of Ibuprofen to the next. The pain was excruciating and the exhaustion that went with it kept me either on the sofa, in my lounge chair on the front porch, or in bed.

By September I thought I could handle the drive to Kane, and the ministry once again but I soon found that my body was not nearly as strong as my mind thought it was. I kept trying but once the snow started to fly, I knew I would have to retire for the sake of the church and for my own sake. They needed a pastor who could meet the needs of the ministry. I needed the winter to recover.

For the last time, I brought my pan of lasagna to the church's traditional Thanksgiving dinner (but that is a story for another book). We had a tearful celebration of our nine years of ministry together.

As the winter months progressed, the snow fell, and then the weather would warm up just enough to form ice and then snow again. The roof of our house was soon weighted down with ice. We hired men from the local Amish community to come and chop away at it, but not before the ice had formed an ice-dam and water had backed up and gotten under the shingles causing it to leak into the bedroom and bring some ceiling tiles down on our bed in the middle of one night.

The men worked for a couple of days and the weather was warming quickly. Before they got to the front of the house, it rained. The rain began late in the night when we were safely tucked in bed. Jon and I had moved to the back bedroom on the first floor. About 3 AM we heard a horrible rumbling sound followed by an explosion.

The ice had slid off the roof, buried itself into the earth in front of both our living room and dining room windows and fallen back into the house. The windows were the lovely old glass made with lead, the kind that really sparkled when you washed them. When the ice hit them, the one in the dining room exploded. The glass shards flew nearly the whole length of the house. The living room window was spared by the storm window but the frame was bent and the glass cracked.

If the rain had come during the day and I had heard that rumbling noise, I know I would have gone to the front window to look out and I probably would have been killed. God had spared us in a very uncomfortable way.

The electric wires for the furnace were cut. There was no heat. The wind began to pick up and the snow came again. Jon searched the basement for plywood to cover the open window. Our son came to help. The furnace got fixed but with the window boarded up, it was a dark in the house and not very warm no matter how much plastic we put over the inside of the window.

We got the glass cleaned up, or most of it, but we always wore slippers or shoes and worried about the dog's feet. And winter settled back in for a couple more months.

The insurance adjuster came and our settlement was a fair one, enough to allow us to hire a contractor who promised to put everything to rights upstairs and down as soon as spring came.

Meanwhile, I cried over the phone to Ginny about how frustrated I was and how I hated winter and just wanted to move to Florida! She seconded that. Florida was the place she wanted to be, as well.

I had never before wanted to move to Florida and Jon just hated Florida. We had visited his uncle in Bradenton once and couldn't figure out why anyone would move to Florida, but one of the men, Corky, I had ministered to through the church in Kane had moved to Venice, Florida after his wife died. He would call and tell me how wonderful it was and my older brother, Norrie and his wife Bev lived in Sarasota and were always inviting us to come down and get out of the cold.

I know it was only by the hand of God and our complete desperation that Jon finally agreed we could fly down and have a *look* at the apartments where Corky now lived with his life partner, Susan. In April, I met my friend Karen for breakfast. Karen and I go back to when she was a little girl and I was her 16-year-old Sunday school teacher. Karen's father, Frank Hagberg, was our pastor at that time. The difference age makes had long since disappeared between Karen and me. Now we were colleagues in ministry and friends.

As she listened to my tale of woe, Karen looked more and more thoughtful.

Finally, she asked, "Becky, have you ever been to Venice? You know that's where Mom and Dad lived."

"No, we've never been there! In fact, it is a miracle I have gotten Jon to agree to go, but we are ready and I just feel this is the place we should check out," I declared with more confidence than I felt.

"Well, would you mind if I told my brother and sisters about your planned visit?"

I thought this was a rather strange request but I agreed that would be fine.

A few days later, Karen called to tell me she had consulted with her siblings and they would like to have us use the home where her parents had lived in Venice Isle Estates while we explored our options in Venice, rested and prayed.

We flew into Sarasota where Norrie and Bev picked us up and then delivered us to Venice Isle Estates.

We fell in love with the town, the park, and the home. Five months later, with our house and contents sold, we moved into Frank and Teedie Hagberg's home.

Then on July 10, 2012, Ginny's husband died. She came to spend some time with us, fell in love with the town, the park and a house just around the corner and down the street from our home.

On April 16, 2013 Ginny moved in to that house. We were nearly neighbors but just far enough apart to allow one of us to get into mischief without the other one knowing!

In God's own time, he had done so much more than we could have ever hoped or even dreamed. Ginny often shared meals with Jon and me. She and I ran around together, went to the jetty to watch the sun sink into the Gulf of Mexico, and were frequently asked if we are twins. It is not unusual for us to meet up to go somewhere and find we are dressed in the same colored clothing wearing similar earrings without ever having consulted on the matter.

Jon used to say his blessing doubled when Ginny arrived. They had a happy, comfortable relationship. Our brother Norrie and sister-in-law Bev get together with us often. We talk with Donna in Bemus Point, NY and with David in Warren, PA and dare to hope maybe one day, in His time, the Lord will bring them here too. My youngest daughter Barb and husband Eric live nearby in North Port. My oldest daughter Kris and her husband and children live in Jamestown, NY not far from my sister Donna. Kris flies down for visits frequently. I chat often with son Jon K who lives in Warren, not far from my brother David.

My adopted siblings both still live in the Warren area. Jim and family came for a visit this summer. I talk with both Debbie and Jim on the phone.

I miss the wonderful family times we had when the house was filled with all our parents, aunts, uncles, cousins, our spouses and our kids. Now all our children are grown up, some married with children of their own and one with a grandchild. Where did all that time go? I thank God for those times and the warm memories whose fragrance sooth and enrich my life.

My double-cousin, best friend Joyce continues to live in Ohio near her daughters and her four young grandchildren. We talk on the phone regularly; our love has only grown stronger through the years and the tears.

I was privileged to serve as interim pastor at Bay Indies Covenant church, located in a neighboring park in Venice, for a year and I am asked to fill in for our pastor when she travels. And these days a lot of the ministry God calls me to takes place through my writing.

I have tried to contact a half-brother and a half-sister on my biological father's side but neither has responded. Perhaps it will happen one day, in God's time.

On April 22, 2017, Jon passed away after a long struggle with COPD. Late in the fall, I met a man while I was enjoying the pool in our park. He was also recently widowed. We began to chat and found we shared so much. Our values were the same and our life experiences were surprisingly parallel. It wasn't long before we realized we were deeply in love and wanted to spend the rest of our days together. On Valentine Day, 2018, we were married in a small, intimate ceremony on the beach.

In July, 2018, my sister Ginny married also. Her husband was also a recent widower and they also met in this park!

Our sisterly love affairs and marriages gave plenty of fuel for the park's gossip line! It also brought a lot of joy to all of us. It still does.

Ginny and her husband Denny have left the park but live in nearby North Port. We are still close in every way.

Habakkuk 2:3 *For still the vision awaits its appointed time; it hastens to the end—it will not lie. If it seems slow, wait for it; it will surely come; it will not delay.*

Baby Becky with Dorothy & Milton Samuelson

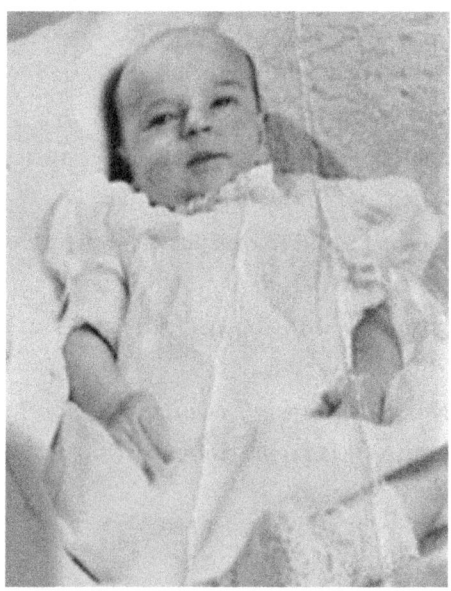

Baby Becky (the original picture found by Donna)

Stepfather Dave Titus and Mom, July, 1965 Wedding
Photo

Becky's "Adopted" family - Debbie, Becky, & Jimmy

Jon & Becky on church steps after their "borrowed"
wedding

Becky's "Found" family: Donna, Norrie, Becky, David, Ginny (July, 1996)

Barb, Jon K, Becky, Kris

The "twins"

Tom and Becky, 2018 Wedding

About Rebecca Erickson

Rebecca was born in Denver, CO, adopted by a family in Warren, PA at the age of six weeks. After graduating from Warren High, she attended Capital City School of Nursing in Washington, DC for a year. She later became a hair stylist and a volunteer Crisis Hotline counselor for the Women's Crisis center in Warren. At the age of fifty-four, she entered North Park Theological Seminary where she earned a Master of Divinity degree, graduating with honors. She and her husband, Tom, currently live in Venice, Florida. She loves to hear from her readers and learn of their stories and how their stories connect with this book.

Email address: beckyerickson357@aol.com

Made in the USA
Monee, IL
05 October 2020